MISS ANGEL

The Evil Behind the Law

Volume I

Tchinda Fabrice Mbuna

Printed in the United States of America

Library of Congress Control Number:		2021902759
ISBN:	Softcover	978-1-64908-849-9
	eBook	978-1-64908-848-2

Republished by: PageTurner Press and Media LLC
Publication Date: 02/16/2021

To order copies of this book, contact:

PageTurner Press and Media
Phone: 1-888-447-9651
order@pageturner.us
www.pageturner.us

DEDICATION

To my mentors,
The dangerously
Anointed and creative
Mind God released
To raise a generation
Of *sans frontiers*
To make the world
Stay as beautiful
As God ever wanted it,
Mr. Awah Oliver Nde.
Dr. Nkongmenec Vivian,
Professor Enongene Sone.

They tickled my spirit,
My heart, my senses,
And all my nerves
In a fearless field of
Creative imagination
Planted in me the skills
Of creative thinking,
Creative construction,
And sarcastic truth speaking
In the most agreeable
And playful manner
Like their inspirers—
Geoffrey Chaucer,
William Shakespeare,
And Bate Besong.

This piece of work is dedicated
To their benevolent rich lifestyle
Of raising heroes for God's world.
Sirs/Madam, here are now
The finest parts of you in me.

FOREWORD

For so many years that I have worked in the field of drama, screenplay and cinema writing, and editing, it has been difficult to come across a rare writer like Mbuna Fabrice Tchinda. He is a writer whose pen smiles like the poetry in his bloodstream.

I found the play so romantic, the language so poetic and philosophical, full of farce, paronomasia, and rhyme at every unexpected level. He is a dramatist and a linguist who surprises even his audience with a desire to stay on. Like Chaucer and William Shakespeare, where the beauty lies is where the satire is born. His language as well is pregnant with humor, which is dangerously didactic. He has a craft of hiding pain in the beauty of sense and emotion in the beauty of language.

It is a poetic play, it is a dramatic play, it is a renaissance play, it is a diasporic play, and it is a play for all ages and societies. A young migrant to Europe, America, Canada, Asia, Australia, or any part of the universe will find himself in the story. Anyone with high expectations from relatives abroad will understand why expectations are not met.

Any person also carried by the beauties of this God's earth shall also find their stand in Miss Angel's exhibition ground while those who wish to become citizens of heaven on this earth will find direction. I dare say the play itself is a research and reawakening center.

It is a play worth watching, it is a text worth reading, and it will be a film worth watching. Universities and high schools worldwide need this play as reference material to illuminate and educate their students on what future awaits them.

—Awah Oliver Nde (Kevnojev)
Writer /Film Director / Producer and Editor/Teacher
Executive Director of Zion Motion Pictures International
Founder of Bethel Films—Cameroon

COMMENTARY

Everything I read from the overflowing pen of the author of this play reminds me of Camara Laye of Guinea-Conakry—one of the most worshipful African novelists of the colonial period. Everything that Tchinda Fabrice Mbuna writes is overwhelmingly autobiographical in context and splendidly artistic in content. He blends romanticism and classism with an unusual *bon sens* and raises both of them to unimaginable heights.

He is the smartest, the sharpest, and the most frugal modern playwright whose work I have had the rare privilege of reading and laughing alone. He does not waste artistic resources. Everything in his distant and immediate surroundings is useful. He catches it in mid-air, brings it down slowly, harvests it judiciously, preserves it carefully, and in due time, he adorns it magnificently. Then, its entertainment delights the heart beyond the ordinary.

Tchinda Fabrice Mbuna has made the writing profession noble, made it admirable, and made it enviable. Nobody will ever regret being a writer, no matter the plenitude of obstacles in his path. His objectivity in reconciling religious hypocrisy and human virtues in this play challenges its traditional orthodoxy and dogmatism of all time. While earnestly grabbing William Shakespeare's gabardine as one of his most faithful pupils, he revisits his medieval predecessor Geoffrey Chaucer. He does not contradict him that *Amor Vincit Omnia* (Love conquers all). With what else than the gift of art can one be ever blessed on earth . . . and in heaven?

—Nkwetatang Sampson Nguekie

The Director (The Writers' Resource and Information Centre Bamenda–Cameroon)

INTRODUCTORY NOTES

Introduction to Diaspora Literature

This play, *Miss Angel,* is classified under diaspora literature. It is literature written by people living out of their respective countries of origin. It is mostly written about the authors' past lives when they were at home, opposed to their new experiences in an entirely different environment. Their past and their present clash and inspire them to reconcile the two by putting it down in writing. Although their current living standards are better than the former, they face many new nerve-racking challenges that sometimes tempt some of them to regret leaving their previous backgrounds and homes.

A motivational writer said, "New level, new devil." Our brothers and sisters think that going abroad in search of greener pastures is very easy. But upon their arrival there, it is very tough. Opposed to the massive unemployment rate at home, they are gainfully employed, they eat well, they dress well, they are healthy, they see good places, they come across people of several walks of life, they learn new things and new cultures, and they open up to the world at large. But all these things only satisfy their flesh. They don't fill their spirit. At this juncture, they realize that there is no heaven on earth.

After being in possession of all these things, people living out of their countries of origin still feel a certain vacuum in their souls haunting them all day and all night long—the yearning for home, the longing to return home, the nostalgic feeling to return home.

Roy Campbell expressed this kind of nostalgic feeling in his poem titled "Horses on the Camargue" as follows:

With coal-red eyes and cataracts mane,
Heading his course for home,
Though sixty foreign leagues before him sweep,
Will never rest till he breathes the foam
And hears the native thunder of the deep.[1]

If horses, which are animals, can be roasted by the irresistible nostalgia fire, how much more human beings? Nowadays, many black American citizens are returning to Africa to trace their countries of origin with the use of their DNA. Some of them landed on the Kribi deep seaport in Cameroon's south region two years ago and celebrated themselves for having originated from Cameroon. Their forefathers were sold as slaves to work in North and South America's sugarcane plantations. That's why many Brazilians look exactly like Africans.

In this play, Tchinda Fabrice Mbuna contends that marriage is not necessarily a bed of roses and acknowledges that living out of one's country is not a bed of roses. There, you must think deeper, work harder, and run faster, or else you will be blown off your track by the wind from the speed that prevails there. If not, one day, you will be mourning like that renegade described by Nkwetatang Sampson in one of his discourses titled "Who Shall Sing Unto Me?" as follows:

Hereupon the streets of San Francisco, I have wandered up and down the hot tarmac for a decade and beyond. Dog-beaten shoes, weather-shaken clothes, skeletal exposed ribs, a vein-woven forehead, and a melancholy-manned countenance. All my school certificates and identification papers got missing in a Baltimore Metropolitan Train. Shortly thereof, I lost my job, and all my businesses crumbled. Today, I have no place to put my head. In misery, I second to no other than Poor Tom à Bedlam. Tears shower my chicks all day and all night

> *long. Tears of sorrow. Tears of impending predicament. Gone are all my possessions. Gone are all my ambitions. Gone are the cool waters of the Colorado Dam. Gone is the Tennessee Valley of roses. Sweet San Francisco and the pleasant Pacific! Oh, gone, are they? I'll never live to see the splendid sun rising any longer. Neither will I ever live to hear the magnificent cockcrow, for tonight, the mortal hands of my ancestors will be raised against me.*[2]

Just entering his fifth year in the USA, the author of this play is sharp enough to realize that if he does not implant his roots at home as quickly as possible, he may one day be a victim of the situation in the extract above. There are many African failures who have lived overseas for more than three decades. For them, returning home is as frightful as hell. They have overfed themselves, drunk milk to the lees, and have become as extra largely baggy as breastfeeding Chicago bulls fattened with alfalfa in a dairy corporation. What will they return and do at home? Where will they live? What kind of work will they do? They cannot do manual labor. They cannot trek. Who will recognize their return? They have eaten and drunk their lives into some kind of protracted illness. They thought they were enjoying it, but today, they see that they were ushering themselves into captivity. They have used their own very hands and mouths in digging their graves. They have themselves to blame.

Diaspora literature is fascinating and enriching because it deals with two cultures and two experiences drawn from two diverse backgrounds and environments—more often than not, the developed and the less developed worlds. You find the author trying as much as possible to reconcile the two experiences and strike a balance to no avail. The following extract from an essay titled "An African's Adventure in America" by Babs Fafunwa is a typical example:

> *Since my arrival in this country to study, I have met over fifty African students during my vacations. I found that most of our impressions after arriving on the American soil are almost identical in exchanging views with them.*

> *Everything about him is new; the student finds out. He is mobbed by a group of inquiring reporters who ask: What is your name? Where do you come from? What is your impression of America? How many wives has your father? Are you married? Is it true that you buy women in Africa? Are you a prince? Is your father a king or a gold miner?*[3]

Notwithstanding the hail of trials and temptations that plague immigrants upon their arrival in their various destinations, they are still better than the local heroes who live and die in their countries without ever stepping their legs out of their frontiers. Traveling is one of the most paramount success principles of all time. Unless you mismanage your physical and spiritual profits from traveling, traveling has always been profitable for all ages.

It is most profitable if you travel and return to where you came from. If you either never return or return in a coffin, it is woeful and regrettable. It can only be celebrated if you are a hero who dies abroad fighting for a just cause. If you travel and die without fighting for a cause, it would have been better if you had committed suicide a thousand times.

TEXT ANALYSIS

The author of this play has given every resident a unique opportunity in his country of origin to see and feel what happens to every young, intelligent man upon his arrival in a foreign country. Rich unmarried women start scrambling to get married to him and even promising to pay his dowry. If he attempts to refuse, they use their wealth and position to mount all kinds of false accusations against him. These women are mostly citizens of that country who are aware that newly arrived foreigners are desperate for jobs, logistics, and legal papers. The earlier they cajole them into their aprons, the better. But unfortunately for them, nobody is above the law. Justice always prevails, and the guilty are punished accordingly.

Miss Angel: The Evil Behind the Law, Volume 1 is a very simple and straightforward play with just four major characters and five minor characters. It can be easily acted on stage without the need for much human and material resources. The author's investment is the message he is passing across rather than in extravagant stage decoration and flamboyant costuming. The audience is learning the tenets of both drama and poetry. He is the protagonist in the play, and in the epilog, he says:

Love is nothing but poetry, prose, and drama

Miss Asunder finds herself in a dilemma. She has failed in love affair several times. Each time she falls in love with someone, he does not equally fall in love with her. Is it a crime for her to love? Should she continue loving, or should she stop loving? Unrequited love is a great tragedy; and in some cases, it is a curse—in the case of the Lady of Shalott in Alfred Lord Tennyson's poem titled "The Lady of Shalott" whose magic mirror cracks from side to side, and she cries:

The curse is come upon me![4]

Does such a curse come upon Miss Asunder? As her name implies, she is cursed to always put asunder what God has put together. Closest to a greater demon is always a lesser demon, inspiring and encouraging his master to perform villainous acts. Such is Lady Macbeth to Macbeth in William Shakespeare's play titled *Macbeth*. Such is Miss Beatrice to Miss Asunder in this play. These two ladies are accomplices in all their plots against Mr. Tchinda. Mr. James and Miss Envy are greedy and mercenary church goers. The author of this play is perhaps one of the last conscience-guided men of God surviving in the church today. Nowadays, all ardent criminals, gold diggers, altar pretenders, and hypocrites have taken refuge under the church's unholy umbrella. And the author has not spared them.

The author's masterful use of the French language in this play identifies him as a typical Cameroonian propagating the culture of bilingualism in a foreign land. Human-made law is corrupt, and man is corrupting God's law. Which law then should we hang on? Tchinda Fabrice Mbuna answers this question. We should hang on to the law of our conscience. It is the only last surviving genuine law, which guarantees salvation for all and sundry.

SYNOPSIS

Miss Angel is an Afro-American love story portraying all allegorical characters except for the protagonist, who lives in the real world. What is the real world—the allegorical stage in which we come to play our role and pass on either with a good mark or a failed mark in the line of destiny.

Miss Angel, a Cameroonian presently residing in America, does her best to fly to her fiancé, Tchinda, who honors her with his love. From the day he enters America, the feminist love fever begins manifesting its greed in him and Miss Angel. In a society where money and legal papers are given more credibility than human life or the fear of God and human integrity, the gates of hell open for them.

With her monetary and Sue Happy Society knowledge and power, Miss Asunder corrupts even close relatives like Miss Beatrice and rooted Christians like Mr. James. The soundness of discernment, gratefulness, and inner godly commitment gives Miss Angel and Tchinda the impetus to carry through.

Miss Asunder spends in many areas since "Money answereth all" and ends up faking a sexual violence scene that drags Tchinda to court on his wedding day. Job's reward becomes his portion after the father of all lies could not find evidence against him as destiny would have it.

They are married before their accusers on the wedding day, with their accusers bound to attend and watch their first kiss. The play is full of poetic oration, romantic attachment, and sincere love feelings. With God, truly, all things are possible.

Miss Angel is a play with a vast stock of artistic beauty and elevating wisdom to be enjoyed by everybody who reads it from the beginning to the end. Set in New York City in the USA, it is about the hail of trials and temptations faced by a young Cameroonian poet upon his arrival in this new world. His stiff resistance to the forces of evil hidden under the umbrella of the law and the church shapes his destiny. His unshakable faith in God saves him.

DRAMATIS PERSONAE

Major Characters

MISS ANGEL—Mr. Tchinda's lover and later wife

MISS ASUNDER—Wealthy American upper-class lady

MISS BEATRICE—Tchinda's former schoolmate, Miss Asunder's best friend

MR. TCHINDA—Cameroonian poet and playwright

Minor Characters

FOUR POLICE (911)—Law Enforcement Officers

JUDGE JUSTICE—The Court Judge (New York City)

MISS ENVY—Mr. James' girlfriend

MR. JAMES—Restaurant attendant (informant)

REV. TYLER—The Priest

PROLOGUE

Apology

This' what I mean to say in my ideology—
There is a point in our feminist liberal theology.
The problem is not with the feminist theology
But in our liberal -ology or ideology.
Every wrong liberal -ology or ideology
Is a wrong liberation -ology or theology.

We all want women's -tion or liberation.
We're all right to fight for our rights,
Sometimes, to be wrong means is to be right.
Sometimes, the best way to be right
Is never trying to always override
Others right when they want their rights.

With due respect, I have for all women,
All women, some wives, mothers to us men,
I believe we are all one, women and men.
I do apologize on behalf of all the men,
To all the female and all the women,
For all the evil we thought and meant
Against them, the torture and the abuse,
Marital rape and female privileges misused.

We men did this in the age of ignorance,

You did suffer Christ-like in perseverance,
Till the feminist law brought you deliverance.
Women, the carrier of divine light and life,
Despite your race, we need you as a wife.
Man is a microcosm within your macrocosm,
We need you by our bosom and handsome
To build this nation and make it blossom.
Let's stand with equal rights as a ransom,
With the law, forgetting fast the past
Looking fast- forward to time that runs fast,
As we hope to a God of gender equality
Let's stand with a faith that is steadfast.

The past is vanity, the future eternity,
The past is futility; the present is unity,
The past was bleak, the future bright.

ACT 1—SCENE 1

NARRATOR

(Off Stage)

In her late thirties, a native of American aborn,
A Caucasian of color, not colored, very pretty adorn!
A fairly tall, curved, and curvy heavy hips,
Well-polished hips, appealing as heart-shaped lips.
With long brown hair lashing her backside,
Her beauty is more than a touristic site.
When she walks on heels, she provokes asides,
From onlookers, men especially with foresight,
Who understand the true haste and taste of beauty.
In a world of beauty contest full of bounty and bootie,
She's a woman of modest goggles who gargles,
And thinks she's so smart because she uses Google,
With extravagant classical mannerism and bangles.

She is a woman of great wealth and great health,
Others call her president of the commonwealth!
She is not only healthily wealthy but ostentatious
But ostentatiously wealthy and healthy in pride.
Her fame in the city is contagious and contentious,
She's pseudo-shrewd, pretentious, and capricious.
She's innocently innocent, dangerous of a bride
For any man who falls into her trap in misguide!

There are many others of her prototype or type
Who dress flashily or flamboyantly in miniskirts,
With long fingernails like beggars at the outskirt,
Who think beauty and sex open every door,
But frail and fail to know, beauty void of character
Is madness, mundanity, vanity, or mere folklore
That fades so sudden as a beauty décor.

She lives in a vast mansion in New York City,
A mansion as vast as the city's capital.
Lights from her mansion, from afar,
Glitter with high immensity and propensity,
Like disco lights from all night clubs in the city.
Despite her grandeur, she can settle for anything less.
She isn't careless, but she cares less, unless
She gets what she wants anyhow less!
Here is she entrapped in her unhappy loneliness,
So desperately stressed, lonely, and loveless,
Watching Hollywood's Romeo and Juliet.
Of the times this fast past, she regrets,
Wishing to have been or be in Juliet's shoe
To have a man she can love and glue too!
A man like Romeo, who can stand on the balcony,
And beg for her love, in truth and even in agony.
Now lost in her thought in despair and cacophony,
Then thinks she of Tchinda, the elegant poet,
As a poet of ambiance who might love some moet,
But he just arrived from Cameroon, March 03, 2010.

Enter Miss Beatrice with much zeal and eagerness,
Her face speaks brightly of hope and merriness.
But what could be that her face lightens up?

She's alike beautiful but of tanned skin color
Who mixes all colors on her face for makeup.
She's Africanly aborn, adorn with no mistake,
She's naturally pretty with well-admired breast,
Supported with textile props to stand at rest!
She's now Americanized in her English accent,
She sometimes speaks English with words so archaic.

She brags of her African decent culture and descent,
Her high heels are as tall as the Empire State Building.
New York City has earned her the name sexy baby,
Perhaps that's why her favorite song is a lullaby.
She only smiles when she's on heat or money needs,
That makes her gentle, polite to hide her misdeeds.
Her eyes can move up and down like a doll,
When she lashes or snubs at you, that's all.
You never think of talking to her again,
Only bourgeoise who are willing for a good bargain
Can make her regain a concealed smile a metaphor!
A Cameroonian, more American than Americans!

INT. ASUNDER'S MANSION - DAY

A mansion of its kind. MISS ASUNDER is sitting so lonely and idle, watching a television love series. Her wooden floor is shining like a newly polished wood with no trace of dust found anywhere. Her walls are decorated blue, and in her loveseat is seen a big teddy bear. She has been drinking a glass of champagne (Dom Perignon). On one corner of her living room is a small bar all stocked with all sorts of Champaign—Armand de Brignac Brut Gold (Ace of Spades, 6 liters), Krug Clos d'Ambonnay, and Veuve Clicquot Yellowboam Ostrich Limited (3 liters).

Even in her nightwear without makeup, she still looks perfect, flawless from head to toe. Her beauty is immortal and can mortify or lure any man to lust. On a glass table standing beside her is a jar of artificially made white and red roses. A spiral staircase to the upper section of the mansion is seen. It is so well made, with imported fabrics. Despite all the elastic grandeur in her disposition or to her pleasure, her mind and heart seem troubled.

Then enters Miss Beatrice.

DOOR OPENS - ASUNDER'S MANSION - DAY

MISS BEATRICE

Did you see the pictures?
So gorgeous with airport structures!
You're so perfect of blend and mixtures,
Only from above can such be found.
Such beauty and love are one of its kind—profound!

MISS ASUNDER

Which—which is which,
Before my heart is bewitched!!
Of course, I am noble and very rich,
But still in the middle of love, deception, or bridge.

MISS BEATRICE

The ones at the J. F. Kenned airport
When Tchinda arrived from Cameroon,
Dressed so hot, jeans, and jack-sport,
His smile and words were soft, vivacious,
A type of man you need, sexagacious,
Always banquet ready—at mid-night moon.

MISS ASUNDER

No!
Where are they, let me devour as a savage,
Before I'm entirely smidgen and ravaged!

Miss Beatrice hands over some of the pictures to Asunder while she steadily admires some.

MISS ASUNDER

(Continues)

He looks very elegant, smart,
And gorgeous! My type, very chubby,
Purple helmeted love warrior, I guess?

MISS BEATRICE

Yes, he is exceptional in virtuosity,
Ambitious, a poet, and a playwright.
So energetic in poetics and vivacity.
Everyone will like to behold and delight.

MISS ASUNDER

Any paramour?

MISS BEATRICE

Not of yet, a paramour, but par amour,
He's admirable by all; let's haste
He's still of fresh blood to face!

MISS ASUNDER

Exception in human history!
Poets' hearts are always full of lust
And never love that one can trust!

MISS BEATRICE

He's different, but If his is full of lust,
Love is what it takes to remedy lust,
From a man's heart who is blind and lost,
To vanity feelings, and deception rust.
You're a woman of great admiration,
Blessed with fairy's beauty to call attention
He's no exception falling in haste or preyed
By the goddess of beauty and all.

She smiles playfully as she picks a chair pillow and throws it at Asunder.

MISS ASUNDER

Lust doesn't prevent love anywhere!

MISS BEATRICE

True love can prevent one from lust.

_Shrugging in disillusionment, she picks up the remote control and changes the Romeo and Juliet balcony scene.

MISS ASUNDER

It could, but not in today's society.
Love always appears like shallow water,
Once in, then you see its insanity.

I have been in, in colder and ones hotter
Than even hell—with men of false piety.

MISS BEATRICE

Wait no longer of the passage of time,
Let not his heart to someone inclined,
It will be hard to then redeem his heart,
Once taken—it can be very hard!

MISS ASUNDER

Men are all sentimental hypocrites.
They put on love as a mask to guise
Their evil intentions, caprices, or vice.

MISS BEATRICE

Nothing else should you dread than fear,
Fear is nothing but an illusion always near,
When good things are about to appear.
Shake off your shackles, let them disappear,
Look into the future; all is possible and clear.

MISS ASUNDER

Can love shackles be off one's neck,
That he lives a love life without any wreck?
Why do fools fall in love and become wise,
Wisemen fall in love and become fools– otherwise?

MISS BEATRICE

We've all been shackled but must move on
Love is a journey; it moves on, even when
You decide to give up; the desire to live on,

Otherwise, you remain in your delusion cage,
And die in self bitterness, distress and rage!

MISS ASUNDER

Love is such an unfateful game!
Others play to win or to make of it a gain,
Others play and get drowned and drained—
Is mine going to be a win or in vain?

Miss Beatrice takes the pictures from Asunder and drops them on the table. Staring at her in the eye, she tries to persuade her by giving her a pat on the back. She pauses. Her eyes were flirting on the channels that Asunder is searching.

MISS BEATRICE

Make love not your enemy nor to blame,
Some men of heart full of misdeeds,
Have made all men look fake or lame,
Tchinda is a nobleman, even in his vein,
Righteousness and true love flows, indeed!
There's no wrong day to be love fallen,
For such love uncommon, are you so stricken,
To let it slip by your eyes to a downtrodden?

MISS ASUNDER

Well—love is still a game of chance.
What of those who fall in love perchance,
On the right day, with the wrong person,
Or fall in love with the right person
On a wrong day?

MISS BEATRICE

Fate is perchance the ultimate answer,
Love isn't so ugly or deadly as cancer.
Don't be so trapped by your failures past,
That you see nothing good or contrast,
Love to anything else, such as an outcast!

MISS ASUNDER

Is love meant for those who don't seek,
Why must those who seek end up sick,
And those who don't find peace and bliss?

MISS BEATRICE

Free your heart; your mind is so displeased,
In love, there's neither a hero nor coward,
We face the same fate; some will increase,
While others will choose to decrease.
Make up your mind to move forward!

MISS ASUNDER

Shakespeare once said,
"Some are born great, some achieve greatness, while some have greatness thrust to them." Could this be my fate?

MISS BEATRICE

Not always the case; fingers aren't same!
Of course, some are born great, like you.
Some achieve greatness and fame,
Others have greatness thrust to them,
Of all this, it only counts 1% inspiration

MISS ASUNDER

Should love be gained or worked for?
Should love be merited, therefore?
Should love be accepted as part of man's fate,
Beyond his will, power, and control?
To fall in love or not to fall in love.
That is where the puzzle lies.

MISS BEATRICE

Suppose the truth about human existence in the face of chaotic circumstances is to be or not to be or to love or not to love. In that case, the question itself is only a test of the human capacity to remain steadfast on what he believes, not what circumstances may cause him to be. However, the truth of being volatile in the midst of circumstances only mirrors one's inconsistency to himself, which by implication means if a man stands for nothing, it is evident that he will fall for everything with hunting and haunting thoughts of being and not to be himself. Chaotic circumstances can only cause a man to grow stronger but not change
What he believes.

MISS ASUNDER

Love is still a stone unturned—
the only axis that rotates men's will power, their fate against their will and wish.

MISS BEATRICE

The only way to be indifferent to others is to be different from their indifferences. Indifference and difference are what make the difference different. Neither does love know such difference nor indifference when it comes to controlling and shaping men's destiny: rich or poor, handsome or ugly.

MISS ASUNDER

Tchinda, I am all alone, so love-smitten,
How do I conquer your noble heart,
To tell you my pains, or stories unwritten?
We will travel together, even to Britain,
To eat love—oh! Where are you to listen,
To a desperate heart, a heart in prison!

MISS BEATRICE

I know you're smitten—be all brave!
Bravery is the strongest fate, sometimes,
To save you from the love you so crave!
Fight for it; don't be to be enslaved,
Victory is yours, all engraved!

MISS ASUNDER

I am braved by women's charm,
Their beauty, their pride to disarm
Any man's heart, but it has failed,
Many times, it left me alone and ailed!

MISS BEATRICE

Love is beauty; beauty is love in disguise.
Discretion is a better part of valor
That controls every love instinct or vice.
Beauty is to love, as a knight to his armor!

MISS ASUNDER

Are we still going to the museum tomorrow?

MISS BEATRICE

A perfect opportunity to win him over!
I have a game plan for you to take-over,
If it works, simple, you see a turnover!
Just watch and see, be braced, hangover.
Until we get him, we must pushover
Just dress sweet, taste good as a lover,
Put a sweet clover cologne; it's our Passover
Your heart shall be pleased with ease!
No more woes, nor thoughts hovering.

They all laugh and share a glass of wine.

EXIT

ACT 1—SCENE 2

NARRATOR

(Off Stage)

Befallen is another nightmare of the night.
Lonely is she, trapped and love-smitten,
Hunted by her thoughts in a wrestling fight.
She's of pleasure tasteless and no delight
She has not chosen to fall in love but is fallen.
O! Slow poison of so-called, she fell in!

She's of the nature zealous and jealous,
Her jealousy is ample to make her love rivals "jailous"!
She has only one dream, to make Tchinda intimate,
Her desires are aflame, just as every mate.
Would she ever have the chance to consummate,
This nocturnal fruit without being a bate?
So mesmerized in dread, pain, and hate,
She hopes to hear him knock at the gate.
Is true love a reality, or should be a debate?
She hugs her teddy bear so dearly as to bear
The trauma of loneliness as it stares.

She's drained of energy, her strength deflates,
Why should night be so unfair for such a fate
To knock at her door in her low state

Despite her affluence, beauty in her estate?

Every now and then, despite her pain,
She struggles to peep through the windowpane.
Hoping for chance, by changer or perchance,
To see him outside the window frame,
But the night grows darker and darker.
The darker the night, the deeper the dagger
Of nonreciprocal love and lustful passion.
Now she's pale in thought and fame,
She will have to spend the night aflame.

INT. ASUNDER'S MANSION - NIGHT

That same night, in her bedroom and bed with her night gown, Miss Asunder is trapped by her emotions and strange desire to have Mr. Tchinda in her arms before any other woman does. Mesmerized in her dreams of falling in love again, she hugs a big teddy bear tenderly just beside her on the bed. Infatuated and desperate, her fingers caress, race, and romance the hopeless bear, and her deep emotions begin to speak to her idle mind and herself.

MISS ASUNDER

What erred for true love to be now managed?
What did corrupt the conscience of love?
Vile men or simply time in its passage?

(smiles to herself and frowns)

Love is a mask for sentimental hypocrites.
Everyone puts it on—well, it's now an adage
Only the brave win, the frail and cowards quit!
Even the virtuous ones—seem all bad or misfit!
Can Tchinda be this noble, real, not counterfeit?

(In a reflective mood)

Should I venture to another unknown adventure?
Well—a dead woman like myself fears no grave.
He doesn't' seem a knave; I need to be brave!
Life is all about risk—a journey of misadventure
Though heart smitten, to a thousand million pieces,
I am the only one to rebuild its broken architecture.

But where do I begin this unknown journey,
Do I begin with fame, beauty, or money?
Men love them all; could Tchinda be virtuous
To deny such pleasures, so sensuous or cernuous?

We control the law and make the world go round,
He will either play by my beauty or law-bound.
I might have failed many times in the past,
Now I know the rules of the game to play fast.
I am ready to deploy my arsenal for a chase
To hunt the only one man deem honorable,
To love a woman, so genuinely and inseparable.

EXIT

ACT 1—SCENE 3

NARRATOR

(Off Stage)

In a lovesick, craving heart is jealousy,
She's by default jealous, no need for an autopsy.
Tchinda, the man she loves and wants,
Here he stands before her, her heart pants,
As they visit a museum in New York City.
Miss Asunder, in her state of pomposity,
Dressed not to address but to redress and reveal
The paradox of what lies underneath her skirt.
She cares not about others' joy or hurt,
Inasmuch as she wins the man, he wants to flirt.
Her dress code is not a public or general alert,
Nor an invitation for onlooker's concert.
She's tactful in her game for emotional gain,
A game that must be played again and again,
To gain Tchinda's admiration and attention.
Tchinda, Cameroonian poet and playwright,
A gentleman of average and lovely height,
Whose voice is Asunder's plight and delight,
His words are few, sharp as a dog bite
When it pieces the heart as a beam of light.
He's also very theo-eloquent and elegant,

With glittering eyes like a crystal ball
Who knows if this what made Asunder fall?
His physique is heavily built like an elephant,
With a wrinkled belly called six-packs.
In between his upper teeth is a gap,
That's why he eats every meat, perhaps!
He doesn't require a toothpick
A charm that makes Miss Asunder lovesick
Whenever she sees him laugh or smile!

She introduces Tchinda pompously to Martin
Her old schoolmate, she once underestimates
In a school meeting, for a date as undergraduates.
He calls himself a black civil right activist
And claims to denounce supremacist
Though he's more of a classicist than an activist.
A man who seeks justice and morality,
Deep in him, he's guilty of sin, immorality.
A lecherous adventurer and puppet,
Who delights in sounding his own trumpet,
In the heat of his desires, sometimes erotic,
He can become so chaotic or poetic
To have a bite of a woman's waste or cake!
Let's retrain here; he's not so fake,
He has some good virtues for issues at stake!
Here is my advice, take the good in him,
Nobody is without errors or supreme.

EXT. NEW YORK CITY - DAY

In a civil rights museum in Manhattan, New York City, articles of civil rights movements are displayed all over the place. Small monuments of Martin Luther King and other civil rights leaders are seen on one corner.

Paintings of mass police murder during civil rights protests are painted mainly on all museum walls. An image of Rosa Parks is seen with the famous historical bus.

One section of the museum has been dedicated to all recently killed blacks by police brutality and the Black Lives Matter activist. These are pictures of Eric Garner, Michael Brown, Tamir Rice, Walter Scott, Alton Sterling, Philando Castile, Breonna Taylor, and George Floyd, with the slogan "I can't breathe."

ENTER TCHINDA, ASUNDER, AND BEATRICE

MISS ASUNDER

(calling Mr. Martin joyously)

Martin!

MR. MARTIN

Hello, Asunder. Nice meeting you again!

Martin, who is putting on museum articles on the shelves, suddenly moves towards Asunder, Beatrice, and Tchinda. He is holding a biography of Martin Luther in his right hand. He embraces Asunder and gives a handshake to Tchinda and Beatrice.

MR. MARTIN

(continues)

Where have you been, my best friend?

MISS ASUNDER

It's a long story. We will have time to talk in detail.

Mr. Martin walks them towards a private guest room in the museum. As they are about to go, Asunder interrupts Martin to introduce Tchinda.

MISS ASUNDER

Martin, please meet my friend Tchinda, a poet and playwright. I am sure you will be good friends.

Martin turns his attention towards Tchinda; then, he smiles as he tries to recall the definition of poetry by William Wordsworth.

MR. MARTIN

Poetry is the "spontaneous overflow of powerful feelings and emotions recollected in tranquility".

MR. TCHINDA

Are you also a poet? You have much love for William Wordsworth.

MR. MARTIN

Not a rhymester of your capacity.

I did some poetry in school but later turn to civil rights activities.

Miss Asunder and Miss Beatrice move to the other side of the museum, admiring new artistic arrivals. Tchinda's eyes begin to race and rest on the wall as he fixes his eyes on Martin Luther's picture on the wall.

MR. MARTIN

Come on. I have a surprise for you.

Tchinda follows Martin from behind as a child would, hoping to get candy for his obedience. They sit at a table. Martin opens up his drawer and pulls a copy of Tchinda's book entitled The Evil Behind the Law, Vol I.

MR. MARTIN

(continues)

I have been reading your book and—

He pauses, then thinks on the day Martin Luther was shot dead, and he nods in disappointment.

MR. TCHINDA

Am I a horrible writer, philosopher, or…?

Staring at Tchinda for a while, he puts his left hand on his shoulder.

MR. MARTIN

(continues)

Tchinda, you're the incarnation of Martin Luther. He was shot dead, but he lives in you. He's alive in you.

MR. TCHINDA

A writer's voice is for his people.
There's much more to be done—

MR. MARTIN

Tchinda, as a civil right and diaspora poet, can you tell me more about your concept of freedom and equality in the present American society?

MR. TCHINDA

I have no other concept of freedom, except that which our forefathers who laid down their lives for America had and dreamt of America today.

MR. MARTIN

Rosa Parks, Martin Luther King Jr., Malcolm, William Edward Du Bois had been American civil rights forerunners. What else have you to say?

MR. TCHINDA

We talk of equal rights only where there is no such word as oppressor versus oppressed, black versus white, etc.

MR. MARTIN

Don't you think civil rights is at the core or has it borne fruits in the American Constitution and other feminist nations?

MR. TCHINDA

These fruits are still premature, and many civil rights efforts need to be carried
Out to mature these fruits.

MR. MARTIN

Briefly, can you tell me what you mean by Luther's civil rights and other civil rights leaders being premature?

Buried in his thoughts about the American black community's future, police brutality, and killings, he nods his head for seconds then begins to recite one of the famous quotes by Dr. Luther Kings.

MR. TCHINDA

"I have a dream that my four little children will one day live in a nation where they will not be judged by the color of their skin but by the content of their character."

MR. MARTIN

Aren't we living the fulfillment of this dream?

(pauses for a while then continues)

Black communities, Africans, Hispanics, Asians, are known to have equal political, economic, and social privileges. What do you think of a post-civil rights nation like America?

MR. TCHINDA

The autocrat had only removed his mask and given the other oppressor to put on and is dancing to the same music before the civil rights movement began.

MR. MARTIN

Who are the autocrats changing masks?

MR. TCHINDA

Luther's civil rights movement only forced white supremacists to relinquish their physical right of sovereignty over blacks or the black community by embracing them in *buses, restaurants, classrooms, hospitals, jobs, restrooms*, etc.—

The feminist law and police brutality have taken over as the new white oppressors, with men taking black negro slaves' position as the *oppressed*—A new Jim Crow regime and hidden police black codes law system.

MR. MARTIN

So sad!
How long do we have to wait and waste?
To reap the fruits of our labor and forefathers?
We fought civil right wars with the same haste
We fought imperial enemies to their face,
We thought we were all running the same race,
But now black lives have to start over again,
To fight for their rights in this racial game,
Called supremacist superiority of fame.
What a vicious cycle of racial cruelty
Black lives matter—this is the reality.

Tears begin to flow down his cheek. He wipes his cheek and continues to gasp.

MR. MARTIN

Martin Luther—shot dead
Malcolm X—shot dead

Abraham Lincoln—shot dead
Michael Brown—shot dead
Trayvon Martin—shot dead
Eric Garner—I can't breathe
Dontre Hamilton-shot dead
John Crawford—shot dead
Michael Brown—shot dead
Akai Gurley—shot dead
Rumain Brisbon—shot dead
Tony Robinson—shot dead
Eric Harris—shot dead
Freddie Gray—shot dead

(Gasping)

Who knows if I won't be the next,
When such a folly only gears to its apex?
Innocent souls shot in their apartment complex.
Our hearts are sore; where is justice gone?

MR. TCHINDA

We cannot build while all bound.
We have seen something so profound
Allow me to say something or expound.
I've seen a black man with a white soul
We all have different skin color, but one blood
We were all born once, and once we shall die
We shall one day stand before him- El-Shaddai
You are not born black by choice
You are not born white by choice
But we have the choice to live as one.
Blacks are now seen as terror and threats.

A tribute to Martin Luther

Meek at heart, shepherded in a black skin,
Like his reformation predecessors,
Luther cried in the streets of Alabama,
Denouncing white supremacy.
A light and a lamb to many, hated with no clemency.

Embodiment of love and compassion of a saint,
Others called him Pastor, Reverend, and Dr. King.
He had been on the mountaintop, as a sane prophet
To predict the world to come, a life full of wellspring.

He was a lion in strength and fearless in words,
Beaten and called outsider agitator, untimely coward,
By his fellow priesthood civil rights brothers or actors.
As gentle as a dove, witty as Solomon, a real pastor!

"The Negro Is Your Brother, 1963" epistolary,
Letter from Birmingham City Jail,
His cry for justice, "Why we can't wait," prevailed.
"injustice anywhere was a threat to justice everywhere."

A nonviolent black activist and pacifist,
Who turned his cheek for his enemies' fist.
He was calm in storm, like a sheep to the abattoir.
A light to the negro, a dreamed for his generation
Light could beget light, he said, in his prediction.

In his homeland, he faced hell for negro redemption,
He called for justice, for the saints with exemption.

He carried his cross daily, went everywhere across.
He came to his Gethsemane, Lorraine Motel—Memphis
An enemy of light, crucified him with a bullet.
And Christ-like, he died peacefully.

America, mother of the brave, now celebrate this hero
Who was not a president in the White House
But remains a landmark on our streets, history,
And third Monday of every January.

Miss Asunder and Miss Beatrice interrupt Tchinda.

MISS ASUNDER

Time is over. We need to be on our way.

The work phone is ringing. Martin exits to answer the phone.

MISS BEATRICE

I hope you had enough fun!

MISS ASUNDER

Of course, I am sure he did. Martin and I have been friends for ten years now. He has similar likes as Tchinda.

MR. TCHINDA

He's a living archive!

MISS BEATRICE

Tchinda,
I have a doctor's appointment.
I will not be driving home with you.
Asunder will have to drive you home.

Miss Beatrice glances at Miss Asunder when Tchinda seems distracted with the hope that Asunder and Tchinda will click together in the course of driving home.

ACT 1—SCENE 4

NARRATOR

(Off Stage)

In a wet weather so unfriendly impaired,
Drive two incompatible love pair—
One is to the other as the West is to the East.
The drizzling evening to some is a snare,
But to others, it a bliss for lovers in Times Square.
Look, she blushes and scratches her hair,
So entangled in emotional affair or despair.
Fear has kept her too long, not to dare,
She keeps on driving in silence to somewhere.
How long can a lovesick heart be scared?
The night is night, streets wet, rosy is the air,
A perfect time to love, moments very rare.
Sometimes life offers us equal fare,
But we fear and dread to make things fair.
As the silence continues and the journey getting near,
Then she finds courage, fearing not to err,
To turn such a blissful night into a nightmare.
When love is a feeling, it needs courage to bear,
When love is courage, there's nothing to fear,
When love is fear, it breeds torture and tears,
When love becomes tears, it leads to wears and tears.

Love is never wrong; it's only a Croix de Guerre.
Love is only wrong; when we make it a warfare,
Rather than living it as it is our welfare.
Finally, she decides to stir the air,
She clears her throat for him to be aware.

EXT. STREET IN NEW YORK - EVENING

Miss Asunder and Tchinda are driving home. The weather is not too friendly through the streets of New York. The drizzling rainy weather makes Miss Asunder more uncomfortable and emotionally unstable, with Mr. Tchinda sitting at the passenger's seat. She begins to blush, speechless for a while, then decides to break the silence after driving some few minutes without words.

MISS ASUNDER

Are you an anti-feminist?

While Mr. Tchinda is still thinking about what to say, Miss Asunder receives an incoming text from Miss Beatrice.

MISS BEATRICE

(texting)

Frail not to fail having fun in abundance.
Propose him a night at your home.
Make of this night a memoir.
You have the keys to the kingdom.
Good luck, girl!

After reading the text, Miss Asunder smiles. A million thoughts are running through her mind. Her heart is panting; her blushing face is becoming more revealing. How long can she resist?

MISS ASUNDER

Sorry,
It was a text of abstraction and distraction.
Nothing—compared to this attraction,
That has lightened me within with passion.

MR. TCHINDA

Sometimes it is a worthy distraction,
It happens to prevent unknown evasive action
That might cause us harm or dissatisfaction.

MISS ASUNDER

Let's come back to full action.
Would you say forerunners of feminism Simone De Beauvoir, Friedan Betty, Angela Y. Davis, and Harriet T. Mill,
Did more harm in the quest for freedom in their civil rights reforms?

MR. TCHINDA

I am a pro-feminist by letter,
Not by law or by-laws!

MISS ASUNDER

Are you anti-post-feminist laws?

MR. TCHINDA

The law isn't a problem to man,
Man has always been a problem to the law.
Post-feminist laws—another "iron curtain."

Or "great wall" of asunder between
African American marriages.

MISS ASUNDER

With the rise of President Barack Obama,
Reviving hopes of black nationalism and trauma,
Are you hopeful of a positive negritude,
Or what's your impression or attitude?

MR. TCHINDA

My awareness hasn't changed its altitude.
My attitude is still same just as negritude
Itself has never changed from its altitude.

MISS ASUNDER

Well—
It means you're part of the trio,
Aimé Césaire, Léopold Sédar Senghor
And Léon-Gontran Damas—negritude
nationalists!

MR. TCHINDA

I'm a Césairean of Aimé Césaire,
"Une Tempête,"—"The Tempest,"
I'm a Senghorian of Léopold Sédar Senghor,
"Black Renaissance and Racism"
I'm a Damasian of Léon-Gontran Damas,
The negro, black or negritude are all verisimilitude,
They still suffer the same fate, police servitude.
The Blackman is still ensnared in racial turpitude.
A modern cobweb, defiling their integral rectitude.

MISS ASUNDER

Consider the Harlem Renaissance,
A cradle for cultural negritude or naissance.
You may as well or be a W. E.B Du Boisian.

MR. TCHINDA

We all stand in the same Césairean tempest,
We must all stand on the shoulder of the past,
To correct our mistakes, presidents, or outcasts,
White or colored, for a hope that lasts.
Conscience is here to remind us of this unrest,
That we all need or desire to see from Congress,
White or black presidents, in the Whitehouse,
Must speak against racism or denounce!
We owe this to our democracy, not demagogy,
We owe this to our democracy, an apology.

There is an incoming call from Miss Angel. He struggles to remove the phone from his left pocket before it stops ringing. He glances at the phone screen and sees the name of Angel. He smiles for a while. She is a dark skin lady in her late 20s who grew in a poor peasant family in Cameroon. She'd eaten French bread so much that she became as slim as the French bread itself. She often smiles modestly and innocently like Mr. Tchinda. Her virgin breasts make her even attractive to Mr. Tchinda and all men in New York City. She is a virtuous woman with short curled and greasy hair who loves dressing in women's pants. She is outspoken, courageous with a peaceful, docile, and delicate appearance. Her beauty is tantamount to a traffic jam when she walks down the streets of Manhattan, New York. The diaspora poet has fallen in love full time with her.

MR. TCHINDA

Please excuse me!

He is talking to Miss Asunder as she struggles to park at her parking lot. Then he talks back to Miss Angel.

MR. TCHINDA

Hello, mon ange!

MISS ANGEL

Hope you have not forgotten?
Our famous poet, so begotten!

MR. TCHINDA

About?

MISS ANGEL

You are the guest artist tomorrow,
Your fans are so eager; you're a hero!

Miss Asunder notices that Tchinda is talking to another woman. Her face drops from happy to sad. Her thoughts fly back to Miss Beatrice's text of taking him for the night. She is confuzzled and morally defeated.

MR. TCHINDA

Oh!—Thanks for the reminder,
It was already off my mind!
I will be there anywhere, before nine.

MISS ANGEL

That's why Angels need angels to entangle.

Tchinda hangs the phone on Miss Angel with a lovesick smile on his face. Miss Asunder calls him thrice before he startles back to himself. Could he be lovesick as Miss Asunder is?

MISS ASUNDER

Who was that, if I might try to ask!
Hope you don't mind if I ask or unmask?

(pauses)

I am sometimes too curious.

MR. TCHINDA

(Smiling to himself then replies Miss Asunder)

She's a she!
Just reminding me of my concert tomorrow.
It would have brought my fans sore sorrow,
If I do not show up for the show.

MISS ASUNDER

You're famous! Fame is contagious.
She must be proud to have you alone!
Just be careful; some women are ruinous,
Hope she's well-seasoned or gracious?

Tchinda smiles and does not reply.

MISS ASUNDER

Well—back to our discussion.

MISS ASUNDER

You still have much hope for change. How can we be better when the Black Lives Movement has become another social ill that calls for another civil rights reform?

MR. TCHINDA

We cannot bring change until change starts by changing the changer.

The only person who can change the changer is the changer.

If you cannot change others the way they think and act, start by changing yourself the way you think and act.

You cannot think and act like the very people you want them to change and expect any change.

MISS ASUNDER

Who then needs to change?

MR. TCHINDA

The congress, the church, "we the people."

MISS ASUNDER

Here is my mansion, we've arrived!
Please, come inside to be revived?
Of such moment, I've long been deprived!

MR. TCHINDA

I would have loved to, but—

Miss Asunder interrupts, feeling sad and gloomy.

MISS ASUNDER

Tchinda, don't tell me no…
Beatrice is not back home yet.
We can spend some time, even get wet
We can spend the night and get whet.
This is your home, nothing to regret.

MR. TCHINDA

Thanks for this unplanned hospitality,
You're so friendly, full of solidarity,
Home is where the heart is.
Besides, I have to rehearse tonight
One of my poem, perhaps a masterpiece,
For tomorrow's awaited performance.

MISS ASUNDER

We can rehearse here tonight.
I love poetry, but I needs some insight,
Together we can incite and recite
Any sonnet, kindle the flame within inside.
Aren't two better than one?

MR. TCHINDA

Unfortunately, Angel is my script.
Only she has the password to unzip.

MISS BEATRICE

She's luckier than being fortunate!
I can also unzip, strip and unstrip—
What if I become the transcript?

MR. TCHINDA

Either transcript or script,
All require a password to decrypt!

MISS BEATRICE

She knows the password,
Can I be the password?
Doesn't it sound pleasant, or right?

MR. TCHINDA

You're right,
Please, give me a homeward ride!
Tonight was a great delight!

EXIT

ACT 1—SCENE 5

NARRATOR

(Off Stage)

So timely in his poetry oration,
In a season when heart's desire attention
And young girls and boys crave for affection.
We've been wounded by love at some point,
All we need for healing is love at gunpoint.
Being hurt once doesn't mean hurt forever,
Falling in love once isn't hurt devoid or never!
Love is a race, not for all those who are swift,
Love is a battle; some have that divine gift,
To win without fighting, nor fall down the cliff.
In the heart of ever, lover is a story to tell,
Others fell, at first sight, some compelled,
Some by manipulation or by a simple spell.
We've all sometimes probed to know what's love,
But it's a mystery not from men but above.
Sometimes we're entangled in it, sort of,
A feeling and pain unique to everyone, kind of,
Delight of a feeling that sometimes we think of,
To be a game of chance that everyone talks of,
Everywhere in the world and poets write of,
Love from their past, present, and future thereof.

They dream to have a perfect lover to be proud of,
True love is true; it does exist but not devoid of,
It's paradoxical, its ironies, metaphors, or sort of,
A mélange that comes together, undreamed of.
We're creatures of love, wired divinely to seek true love,
A burden in human hearts difficult to get rid of,
Especially if once been hurt of what we got hold of,
Thinking to be all perfect, like a mourning dove.
In our poet's heart is a love poem, let's be abreast of,
Let's hear about his fears and the likes of,
What's true love and how to take hold of,
I will regain my silence and let him speak off.

EXT. TIMES SQUARE, NEW YORK CITY - EVENING

There is an art contest in Times Square Theatre Hall in New York City, where Tchinda is invited for a stage performance. He does a brilliant performance to please his audience.

MR. TCHINDA

(enters)

A Bed of Roses

I thought life was a bed of roses.
I saw a bed of roses without roses.
I asked myself, "When shall the roses grow
When the laborers live in sorrow
And can't fathom the mystery of tomorrow?"

All is vanity, and vanity is life.
I said when I grow old, I will have a wife,
But I know of a couple which lived in a pair
But today, the one-time Romeo and Juliet

Now live in pairs, impaired and in despair.
I believe Romeo was never wrong
To die by Juliet when he thought she was gone.

Life can be a bed of roses,
But hardly will you find a bed with roses.
If I were to love and have a wife tomorrow,
Will my bed be that of roses or sorrow?
Life is unfair, and love is unpredictable
And brings more pains unforgettable.
But poetry—
A bed of roses that makes you comfortable.

The only lover that you can love and trust
And your love will never rest, not rust,
Like Romeo thought Juliet was rusting,
But she was only resting,
And both ended up resting and rusting,
And when you rest, you rust.
If I forsake my love for poetry for a wife,
Will Romeo's fate befall me in life?
But every manly man must have a wife,
Lord, save us! Lord, save us!

There is applause and yelling from the audience.

EXIT

ACT 2—SCENE 1

NARRATOR

(Off Stage)

There's no perfect way to fall in love or be free of,
Not ever falling in love or not being sick of,
Falling in love and later be neglectful of or dispose of.
A love affair so enshrined in what's called young love.
When Miss Angel, beyond her will power, admits of,
That she's been so deprived of love, even barren of,
Until she hears and sees Tchinda's fear to get out of
What's most dreaded by all or fall short of.
There is no perfect day to fall in love, which consists of,
Just falling in love, the day, it comes and let go of,
Our pride, pains, fears, and empty ourselves of,
Anything of our past so undeserving or worthy of,
Getting us to the bliss of love, nor permitting us of
Or allowing us off, breaking off the destitute of,
Anger, bitterness, malice, jealousy, and indicative of,
The fragilities and frailties of humanity, suggestive of.

EXT. NEW YORK CITY - SAME EVENING

Outside the theater hall, as people greet Mr. Tchinda, Miss Angel catches up with him and starts up with him in French. Miss Asunder secretly comes to watch the performance. She hopes to catch up with

Tchinda just after the performance, but she cannot because of the crowd. Miss Angel is swift to make her way to meet him. Miss Asunder, buried in the crowd, watches from afar as Tchinda and Miss Angel get more intimate. She is growing more jealous and bitter.

Streets and the moonlight are shining.

MISS ANGEL

Rêve-je?

MR. TCHINDA

Non!

MISS ANGEL

So soon—have you become famous,
As a poet and playwright, so sagacious
In the local newspapers and media?
What a living encyclopedia!

MR. TCHINDA

A man's gift makes way for him—
And takes him before kings.

MISS ANGEL

A poet—when did you become?

MR. TCHINDA

When I first fell and felt I was in love.

MISS ANGEL

I do still believe not mine eyes,
It's a dream—beyond just a surprise!
When I first heard it from some guys!
I thought it was just guys playing some guise!

MR. TCHINDA

Be not the second doubting Thomas.
Though it has been a long—time past!

MISS ANGEL

To me—
You did say silence; you were a poet!

MR. TCHINDA

Should the baby's coming be a surprise When a woman is pregnant?

MISS ANGEL

Little did I know you were pregnant—And for whom, if I may ask?

MR. TCHINDA

An unknown angel!

MISS ANGEL

Lucky enough, I am an angel, but that angel—am I lucky enough?

MR. TCHINDA

If a man doesn't plan to fall in love—
Love will plan to fall in love with him.

MISS ANGEL

Who then is fallen?

MR. TCHINDA

Both love and I—
We all fell in love when we felt in love.

MISS ANGEL

If I can't get the object now, can the shadow at least be mine that I may fan my hopes and wait for that time in the stillness of silence?

MR. TCHINDA

As you solely desire, miss, but there is no shadow without an object, nor shelter in the absence of a shadow. True love is never amiss.

MISS ANGEL

Why is fate being so unfair to me?
Why do others fall in love, and see stars,
And when I fall in love, all I can see are scars?

MR. TCHINDA

Fate, without faith, will soon fade. Love is a star, but true love begins with a scar.

MISS ANGEL

What then is the price to pay to get both the star and the scar?

MR. TCHINDA

Love has thorns, and thorns have love—
Both are priceless.

MISS ANGEL

If this won't ail you, can I, as from today, call you mine, if you don't mind? A heart that bleeds, bleats, and beats never sleeps but always leaps.

MR. TCHINDA

Perfect love casts out fear. Only love can turn a coward's fear into a hero's fiercest spear.

MISS ANGEL

As it pleases you, I will watch in prayers. Perhaps the sun may rise on my roof—
Oh! Sun, be noble to my prayer.
I beseech you; I am melting within!

MR. TCHINDA

Love is like the sun that always shines—
Don't wait for the blazing and razing rays
To know it has been shining.

MISS ANGEL

Sweet Jesus! Is love woebegone??

MR. TCHINDA

No, it isn't—it has only begun!

MISS ANGEL

You can kill two lovers—
But never their love. It's eternal.

MR. TCHINDA

Please don't arouse love,
Until he does so desire, love is like the beauty of a sleeping baby. If aroused halfway, it may roar like the ocean wave—to overflow and floods its banks.

MISS ANGEL

Farewell, my mind and mine, and I will fail you for not picking your calls in my midsummer night's dreams.

MR. TCHINDA

Love is the only friendly enemy of man—
Man is the only enemy friend of love.

He turns his back to depart.

MISS ANGEL

Are you so soon departing—
When my heart within is still darting?

Your love is so imparting?

MR. TCHINDA

Yes, any other love party?

MISS ANGEL

Not party, but healthy hearty!

Would you mind signing out on my jaw with the gentle ink of your lips before departing that I may know I met you?

MR. TCHINDA

A kiss is dangerous—

It speaks for the heart when words have lost their potency or equipotency!

MISS ANGEL

A kiss from a loved one is a flower—

Whose root is planted deep in the heart,

Only in the heart can it be watered, nurtured to mature!

MR. TCHINDA

Of a kiss, some people fall in love,

before they love—others love before they fall in love by a kiss and for a kiss.

MISS ANGEL

Which fall is your original fall?

MR. TCHINDA

Both the fall before and the fall after—
All is that there is a fall and not my fault.

MISS ANGEL

The fall isn't only your fault, nor is it my fault that we've all fallen in this fall.

MR. TCHINDA

To fall in love is a fall for fun—
To fall out of love is a fall of fun.

MISS ANGEL

It is better a fall for fun—
Than never to have fallen fond
Of any love, fun. Your love inspires me.
The more I love you, the more I am inspired.
I love you so much, but my only fear is the more I love you, the more I will be very happy.

MR. TCHINDA

(reciting a farewell poem)

No Love, No Lover

I have heard stories of people in love,
I have seen people fall in love,
I have even seen people fall out of love.
What does it mean to be in love?
How is it going to look like when I fall in love?

Would it look like a sweet story in a dream,
Or as short-lived as a piece of ice cream?
If I ever fall in love, who is that fortunate one?
What will she really want of me?
Will she need a kiss, a hug, or an embrace?
Or merely a lovesick man and brace,
To say I love you eye to eye and face-to-face?

It is possible to know when one is in love,
But impossible to know whom the heart shall love.
A man may fall in love,
But it takes the heart and the eyes to agree,
Even if the emotions and reasoning are angry.
There's no difference between a heart, lovesick and hungry.

If God our Creator is love and a lover,
Then He must have somebody to love and a lover,
And who is that love and lover?
God himself is lovesick and needs somebody to love
You and I are the persons He wants to love.

MISS ANGEL

Love is the only confusion that should not be confused with the real confusion.

MR. TCHINDA

L'amour est un don de grâce, A toute race, pour rendre grâce, **À** son Créateur, le donateur.

MISS ANGEL

Que l'homme ne sépare donc pas ce que Dieu a uni.

MR. TCHINDA

Amen!

There is an incoming call from Miss Beatrice to Miss Asunder.

MISS BEATRICE

(on the phone)

Did you get the target?

MISS ASUNDER

Misfortune and calamity, was I born!
A mischievous adventure again!
There she is, smiling with the man I love
Not conscious that I am here in pain,
Not feeling that I feel lonely in chagrin.
Is this an evil spell, an omen for misadventure?
I have become an adventurer of tragedy!

MISS BEATRICE

Calm down and count down!
You might be down, but not know-down
Solace, let me define this noun
Tchinda is just a clown-
Whose pride must meltdown.
There is just one Rome,
But many roads… the shortest might

Not be the fastest, but we will get there.
Solace, let me define this noun
Tchinda is just a clown-

The call then ends.

EXIT

ACT 2—SCENE 2

EXT. HARLEM, NEW YORK CITY - DAY

An hour later, in Miss Beatrice's apartment, Mr. Tchinda enters, lovesick. Miss Beatrice has been impatiently waiting for him to come.

MISS BEATRICE

Have you eaten all day long?
Your day has been so prolonged—
I thought something went wrong!

MR. TCHINDA

Food is for the stomach—
And love is for the heart.
But love conquers every hunger.

MISS BEATRICE

What anguish eats the flower on your brow that it has suddenly grown pale with anxiety?

MR. TCHINDA

Not food famished anguish—
The hunter is hunted—
I am haunted!

MISS BEATRICE

It sounds like a game.
Have you been gamed for gain,
Or still a bargained game?

MR. TCHINDA

Even if it was a game—
I am a hunted game,
Beyond my words or fame—

MISS BEATRICE

Who hunts and haunts you?

MR. TCHINDA

Love, how noble is your nobility?
Love, how cruel is your cruelty?
Love, a flower of nobility and cruelty
Yet with a delightful poison.

MISS BEATRICE

Stop sobbing—be sober!
If you are a wounded game,
Don't allow it to cause you lame.
Love doesn't respect fame—
Fame brings pride, but love is a flame.
That tests the pride of every fame.
Don't feint to faint into shame!

MR. TCHINDA

It is so deep and woeful.
If poetry could suffice solace,
I would have written more and more.
I need Angel; I need an angel,
Call Angel for me, my only angel.

Miss Beatrice is on her knees, with eyes closed.

MISS BEATRICE

(mumbling some words of prayers)

Gracious Father,
Open his eyes to see the angel—
The angel of fortitude of Gethsemane.
He has eyes but cannot see.
He has ears but cannot hear.
I have played him a flute to dance,
But he cannot dance to it.

Tchinda exits unseen or unnoticed. Then Miss. Asunder enters.

MISS ASUNDER

What is it that kills the pride of your knees, that you pray not to fall prey?

MISS BEATRICE

Man is nothing without God, and God is nothing without man. God's joy is fulfilled in man, and man's joy is fulfilled in God.

MISS ASUNDER

I have never known you as a Christian.

MISS BEATRICE

Never judge the devil in the morning,
for he might have become a saint overnight.
(pauses then gets up from her knees)
Does the Bible not also say,
"Judge not, and you shall not be judged"?

MISS ASUNDER

God regretted to have made man.
Have you ever read the Bible?
Did Satan repent for being ousted from heaven?

MISS BEATRICE

Christianity is not a title, but a providential responsibility of the Father and His sons

MISS ASUNDER

Mr. Tchinda is my responsibility.
Where is he?

MISS BEATRICE

He was here a while ago, perhaps. He has gone to an unfamiliar garden by himself and for himself.

MISS ASUNDER

Which angel did take him out?

Which Garden of Eden can they be?
What can they be doing there?

MISS BEATRICE

No angel was here with him.
He was lonely, alone, and lonesome.

MISS ASUNDER

Even though the tortoise walks very slowly, don't think that she thinks as slowly as she walks.

MISS BEATRICE

Auspicious and propitious are suspiciously suspicious, but auspicious and propitious are suspiciously unsuspicious.

MISS ASUNDER

You might not have seen the visible
Angel, but I am sure the invisible
Angel present here took him out,
And he may come back invisible.

MISS BEATRICE

Why let your heart pant in fear?
If you can't face your fears,
Your fears will never fear to face you.

MISS ASUNDER

A rat should never call a cat his twin brother simply because they live in

The same house—so is love.

MISS BEATRICE

Only a despairing rat ran for refuge in the dwelling of a caring cat.

MISS ASUNDER

I wander and wonder if he feels
the way I feel, think the way I think,
desires me the way I desire him
love me the way I love him to hell?

MISS BEATRICE

Circumstances may cause one to love out of his will.

MISS ASUNDER

Your will may as well cause you to love out of your circumstances.

MISS BEATRICE

To love is insanity, and to be loved is the only antidote. The only reason why people fall in love is that they do not know why.

MISS ASUNDER

I might not know why,
But I know I feel it wide and wild!

MISS BEATRICE

It's worth the strength of a thousand battalions, when you feel and are filled

With the same feeling, you feel.

MISS ASUNDER

When a man has fallen in love, would you also blame him for losing his senses?

MISS BEATRICE

Not with all his senses and sensibility.

MISS ASUNDER

When love and passion do not meet on the crossroad, it is the heart that suffers.

MISS BEATRICE

Hard times.

MISS ASUNDER

Beggars have no choice in a strange land, nor should they be choosers. I will take to my heels but let him know I came.

(shrugs)

MISS BEATRICE

With the feminist laws, women do not need microphones to speak at a town-hall meeting.

MISS ASUNDER

The law is the mouthpiece of every dumb woman.

MISS BEATRICE

Be still and depart in peace.

Every desperate rat always seeks refuge in the dwelling of a cat. I am the cat.

He is the rat!

MISS ASUNDER

Don't forget that we live in a sue-happy society, where mice have learned how to pursue cats.

MISS BEATRICE

To love is a sacrilege—

To be loved is a privilege.

EXIT

ACT 2—SCENE 3

NARRATOR

(Off Stage)

Give it to me; I love it wild,
Give it to me wild; I love it wide,
Give it to me wide, don't ask why,
If you ask me why, I know I am shy,
If you ask me why shy, I don't know why,
Give it to me wild; I don't know why,
Give it to me wide; I love it wild!

It doesn't matter how wide, wild, or its height,
You're a good guy to say goodbye when days go by.
You can call me your baby then sing for me a lullaby,
Give it to me wild; let me moan, groan, and cry,
Don't ask me why, don't tell me buy or bye.

You're the one my eyes admire, and my heart desires,
I will feed you with wild grapes when you stop by
As nights go by, love amplifies these desires,
To have you, to squeeze you, to share my pie,
With you alone, in the open, in secret, or run by,
And to every one of my love for you in an outcry.

The sky is empty of clouds; it's beautiful, its July
What else? Come by; let's eat some pie or comply
With the demands of love, against all oath, let's defy,
That which man has made, I love me guy.

Give it to me; I love it wild,
Give it to me wild; I love it wide,
Give it to me wide, don't ask why,
If you ask me why, I know I am shy,
If you ask me why shy, I don't know why,
Give it to me wild; I don't know why,
Give it to me wide; I love it wild!

If you choose to make me a slave, I will abide by!
My heart is vacant; only you can occupy,
Remember when I saw you dressed in a bow tie,
Just like in days of old, our high-school style.
How times flies, but memories do not die!
Since love is secret, let's consummate on Mount Sinai,
Where no one can see us, nor chase us in decry.

INT. MISS ANGEL'S APARTMENT - LATE NIGHT

Mr. Tchinda is knocking at the door. Miss Angel peeps through the door in her nightgown and sees Tchinda standing. She adjusts her bra to shoot up her pointed breast towards heaven. Her see-through white lace nightgown exposes her curved hips as sweet as her lips. Tchinda then enters. His eyes are fixed on her curvy backside that keeps him agape. He is staring speechlessly and is motionless for a while. Both hearts panting, eyes interlocked. Thoughts gyrating their minds with paradoxical fantasies of pleasure.

MISS ANGEL

Come in well!
I can't anymore resist your spell!

MR. TCHINDA

What makes an angel so weep,
When you needed to be fast asleep?
What woes you with wet tears so deep,
Making you drain and waste?

MISS ANGEL

I was praying.

MR. TCHINDA

Sorry to have interfered—
Little did I know you were praying.
Instead, I should have gone playing.

MISS ANGEL

You here on time, you did well,
To solace me from this love spell.
I have so fallen to dispute or repel.

MR. TCHINDA

Did you pray for me or against me?

MISS ANGEL

Neither for nor against you, but for us.

MR. TCHINDA

If my angel is praying, then I believe the Sanhedrin of angels is gathered in heaven in prayers.

MISS ANGEL

What love cannot do, prayer can do.

MR. TCHINDA

For whom are you praying?

MISS ANGEL

I am praying for my heart not to fall prey.

MR. TCHINDA

Why should an angel be scared,
When she is the only flower in the garden?
The one and only in Eden!

MISS ANGEL

We live in a sue-happy society.
Things are done with anxiety—no pity.
Many fall in love to survive,
Some revived to fall in love and survive!

MR. TCHINDA

If a rose flower is a flower—
Then all roses are flowers.

MISS ANGEL

All roses are flowers, but not all roses
Are flowers in America—
Under the feminist laws, white roses are Black and black roses are white.

MR. TCHINDA

If you be the only rose, I have found, shouldn't I say you are a garden of flowers, a flawless flowering flower in my garden?

MISS ANGEL

Every flower has beauty, but not Everybody sees beauty in every flower. How come your garden is called mine?

MR. TCHINDA

A rose by any name remains a rose.

You are that rose in my heart a long time Ago when we used to be kids—

MISS ANGEL

Right per chance,
But not in a strange land as such
Where true love is an occasional episode
In a drama of pain, lawsuits and despair.
Love pairs yesterday are now impaired
That's our society and the normal code!

MR. TCHINDA

That's their code, if you won't mind,
Can I call you Miss Rose Angel?
Your worth is immeasurable, divine!

MISS ANGEL

You now have the keys—
To enter my garden at peace and ease.
Call me Mrs. Rose Angel Tchinda .
If that suffices you being my hero!

MR. TCHINDA

Love without marriage is unfinished.
Marriage is what makes love polished.

MISS ANGEL

I am ready for your demands and wish,
I am to your love's mercy as a sandwich,
To be eaten in either love or marriage!

MR. TCHINDA

Would you accept to be my bride?

MISS ANGEL

So alright!
It's my bride's pride,
To give up, even my birth right,
For such a love, admired with delight.
The flower, the stem, the roots belong

To the gardener, not to the tree alone.
I will marry you in heaven and hell.

MR. TCHINDA

Who then is the gardener,
And who then is the tree?

MISS ANGEL

You are the gardener, and I am the tree.

MR. TCHINDA

Blessed be your garden.
Blessed be the flowers they will produce.

MISS ANGEL

Blessed be the gardener who plants,
There is no garden without a gardener
To care for.

Tchinda recites one of his poesy orations to Miss Angel.

A Time When Flowers Blossom

In every garden, there is a gardener.
There was once a garden.
In this garden, there was Adam and Eve.
And there was a gardener.
This gardener was God.

If I truly have something to tell you,
That will be in a garden.

If I truly have something to tell you,
Let time create time.

And I will know what to tell you.
If I truly have something to tell you,
Let patience make us more patient.
And I will know when to tell you.
Let time and patience mingle,
And I will know how to tell you.

I truly have to tell you something.
Let's wait for time to time us,
And I will know what to tell you,
When to tell you, how to tell you,
Where to tell you, what I truly have to tell you.

What I truly have to tell you,
Is still on the wings of time.
Let time create time.
Let patience create patience,
For our flowers to fully blossom.
We shall then have our own garden.
We shall be Adam and Eve the second.
We shall also have a gardener.
And God will be our gardener.

MISS ANGEL

Men fall in love with what they see,
And women by what they hear.

MR. TCHINDA

What have you heard that has made you fall in love?

MISS ANGEL

I have heard just all that can make a woman fall in love.

MR. TCHINDA

Love is the only sin without any redemptive price.

MISS ANGEL

The only redemptive price for sin is love.

MR. TCHINDA

Then, love and redemption are two lovers who can only live together and forever in Eden's Garden.

Miss Angel plugs a stem of an artificial branch of a rose flower from a jar standing on her table and gives it to Mr. Tchinda as he moves towards the door to leave.

MISS. ANGEL

Flowers do not have mouths to speak,
Yet they are always in love and married with bees.

MR. TCHINDA

Your flower has said all that you have to say. Give me not the gift but give me the giver.

MISS ANGEL

She is yours, forever and ever.

MR. TCHINDA

Amen!

MISS ANGEL

Now that you have the giver, take at least the gift. Today is February 14, a day for *Mr. Valentine* and *Mrs. Valentine.*

MR. TCHINDA

You cease to be called Miss Angel.
Miss Valentine is your second name.

MISS ANGEL

Whatever name pleases you, my king,
Call it, to the pleasure of my soul,
Which delights to hear you coo or sing!
I am ready for you to sing; let me sink!

Kissing each other passionately.

The rest is history.

EXIT

ACT 2—SCENE 4

NARRATOR

(Off Stage)

You need not fall from heaven to find love that dares,
Love is to everyone who wants it, or who cares,
Love is glorious to what else does it compare?
To the stars, moon, or sun? Let him be joyous in tears
Let a lovesick that finds love merry to marry
Love sometimes awaits all days and night or tarries,
Just to meet the perfect one whose love is and airy.
Love is a highway; drive slowly, do not be in a hurry,
He that drives fast misses his exit, sometimes scary.

Love is a broad lane; no one way to love; it varies,
Others fell in love yesterday, others today, or tomorrow,
When is not the problem, we all have the same race to race,
Others might choose to race fast, haste to face disgrace,
Others have seen it the hard way, that love is like a staircase,
You get into it one step a time, not for fun or showcase,
However, to find joy, peace, happiness, and embrace.
A newly love-stricken heart is of noble kindness or ease,
True love comes in when two lovers find a commonplace,
Where they can feel happy, joyful, anywhere and anyplace.
Love is a cyberspace, difficult to explore but very possible,
Possible when you find the right person whose database,

Is of true love like Miss Angel's love, simple, plausible.
I am glad Tchinda's in love, but love has a fireplace,
It's where hearts are refined, love tested for the impossible.
Trust not a heart that hasn't been tried for love everlasting,
It might begin as a fire so wild but, in the end, misfire.
I bet you all, I have seen many cases, and I am forecasting
That my hero of a diaspora poet Tchinda might go fasting.
True love is never smooth, but it is worth falling,
Sometimes it never rains but pours, to make you crawling,
I'll support Miss Angel, who's lovesick and hears love calling,
She will fight with her might to preserve it from dropping,
Even if it hurts and requires some blood dripping,
The drama of trauma has just begun wailing and sprawling.

INT. MISS BEATRICE'S APARTMENT - 1:00 AM

Mr. Tchinda enters. Miss Angel's kisses have brightened his face. His heart is merry to marry her when the day comes. His lips are playing the endless melody as the night sings silence. His heart still panting in flashback, with past memories making him to grin from time to time while nodding his head for self-courage.

MISS BEATRICE

Have you been to a garden?
I see your face so ardent and gladden!

MR. TCHINDA

Of course!

MISS BEATRICE

Who's Eden?

MR. TCHINDA

Angel's.

MISS BEATRICE

Oh!
Haven't you made up your mind—
Is she your gardener or pardoner?

MR. TCHINDA

Yes, the African queen!
We knew each other back home,
She's my only garden—Eden!

MISS BEATRICE

America is a land of opportunity—
But there's a game in the community!
Play it by the rules or be ruled and played!
opportunity for the people of the land who are law-abiding.

MR. TCHINDA

The rule or law rules over its citizens,
But love is above all laws and rules,
And doesn't need congressional approval,
Except that of the conscience!

MISS BEATRICE

Miss Asunder is a lavished bride,
She's all men's dream, desire, and pride.
She has it all, love, cars, and money.
She loves you more than any angel would,

She's willing to feed you with wild honey,
Angel can be venomous—of no good

MR. TCHINDA

Hold your peace over my angel,
I see your conscience is so corrupt,
The conscience of my heart is incorrupt.
Neither can money buy, interrupt
My love for Miss Angel.

MISS BEATRICE

Be of gentle spirit; I know you still fresh,
And needs time to think or refresh.
We're all migrants, with stories to tell.
This land is good, but one can't foretell
What might happen tomorrow

MR. TCHINDA

Angel is of my color and blood,
A lizard in Cameroon, Africa,
Can never become a crocodile in America. A crocodile in America will never become A lizard in Cameroon, Africa.

MISS BEATRICE

In the absence of a crocodile,
You can still manage a lizard.
That's a natural law.

MR. TCHINDA

If Angel is not a crocodile yet,

I can manage her as a lizard!
I can't be intimated into an illicit relationship of which I do not solicit.
Miss Asunder rich, but somehow uppish!
Miss Asunder is pretty, but also braggish!
Miss Asunder has the papers, but brutish!

MISS BEATRICE

Beggars have no choice,
Once in a foreign land.
She's all the odds, but has the upper hand,
To control the law for us to expand.

MR. TCHINDA

You're right; beggars can be choosers,
Not always looked upon as losers!
I have chosen Miss Angel and not her.
America is the land of freedom—right?
Freedom for everyone in the land
Both whites and blacks alike.

MISS BEATRICE

Can you please do me a favor,
Which will work for our pleasure
Here is a land of all earthly treasures,
You can enjoy it beyond all measures,
If only you know the way to this leisure.

MR. TCHINDA

Which of the wish is your favor?

MISS BEATRICE

Marry her.

MR. TCHINDA

When love loses its savor,
It also loses its favor.
Love is a treasure and only few can find,
Once they find, there is a price or fine
To nurture it alive and well refined.

MISS BEATRICE

At times, one must forgo his
Savor in favor of his favor!

MR. TCHINDA

So, I have forgone her with all her savor,
I've chosen angel as my favor.

MISS BEATRICE

Amend and emend your speech,
They're all beautiful ladies each,
Papers and money speak louder
Does this not sound to you more lauder?

MR. TCHINDA

Money can bribe the heart into marriage,
But can't buy a man's heart to love in marriage.
True love has no monetary value.
It's neither of white supremacists,
It's neither for racists nor classicism.

MISS BEATRICE

The key to your success is in my hands,
Of course, I have made for us good plans
To make of America our dreamland
But you make of these plans and drift-land

MR. TCHINDA

If you fool me once,
You make yourself a fool;
If you fool me twice,
I make myself a fool.

MISS BEATRICE

Fools are wise in their eyes,
They delight to be wise and strong.
They don't listen to counsel to come along.

MR. TCHINDA

We all have one home—
Heaven where there isn't weak nor strong
The strong are the weak, while the weak are the strong

MISS BEATRICE

Let's live reality here in America,
Heaven is a dream of cowards hereafter.
America is not for the faint, but brave,
The faint of heart, like you, see it a grave!
That's why you behave just like a slave.

Miss Beatrice gives a sarcastic look to Tchinda then continues.

MISS BEATRICE

I will give you time to think.
If you think well with time,
Many things will come with time.

MR. TCHINDA

I think for time,
Time does not think for me,
Nor can it make me unthink,
My love for Miss Angel.

There is a phone call from Miss Asunder to Miss Beatrice. She has been helpless on her bed, unable to sleep. She is lonely and wishes to talk with someone.

MISS ASUNDER

Hello, girl!
Any mannas to kill the void in my heart?

MISS BEATRICE

Still hoping for mannerism to born.
We cannot give up so soon.

MISS ASUNDER

How is Tchinda? Is he at home?
Can I just hear his voice for solace?

MISS BEATRICE

He is with me and by me.

MISS ASUNDER

Please. Can he talk?

MISS BEATRICE

Talking with him or talking to him?

MISS ASUNDER

Talking to him and talking with him.

MISS BEATRICE

Okay, wait a minute!

She gives the phone to Mr. Tchinda.

MR. TCHINDA

Hello!

MISS ASUNDER

Greetings from a heart pale as night. Speak soft to me, O Poet of my dreams, That I might have a night of dreams.

MR. TCHINDA

Only good hearts have good dreams.
Think right, and your dreams will be right.

MISS ASUNDER

Can you mingle tonight?

MR. TCHINDA

Tonight won't be possible
Every other night, implausible!

MISS ASUNDER

What about tomorrow noon,
To eat some good raccoon?

MR. TCHINDA

Incongruously impossible—implausible!

He gives the phone to Miss Beatrice.

MISS ASUNDER

Tchinda is a clown,
Meet me home, for the club downtown.

MISS BEATRICE

No problem, we'll crack him down!
No problem, we'll trap him down!
(drops the phone)

Miss Beatrice exits to meet Miss Asunder. There is an incoming call from Miss Angel to Mr. Tchinda.

MISS ANGEL

Hello, my king. Happy birthday!

MR. TCHINDA

Thanks, my queencess!
You're priceless!

MISS ANGEL

Any up-coming plan?

MR. TCHINDA

You're my plan, my plan planer!

MISS ANGEL

Then—
I have you for myself the entire day!
I'll be picking you up without any delay.
Just be ready; I'll call once on the way.

He hangs the phone. His thoughts begin to speak to him as he joyfully runs to take a shower.

MR. TCHINDA

Even now, I am ready for a relay,
I can't wait to inhale your spray,
Let my heart in your arms swing astray.

MISS ANGEL

Are you this lonely tonight

MR. TCHINDA

Not just lone, lonely alone!

MISS ANGEL

Can I come over,
Pick you up, to sleepover?

MR. TCHINDA

I am at the mercy of your gentleness
Come over, let's sleepover,
And let mid-night love take over!

EXIT

ACT 2—SCENE 5

INT. MISS ASUNDER'S MANSION - DAY

Miss Beatrice and Miss Asunder are planning to go out for dinner.

EXT. TIMES SQUARE, NEW YORK

MISS ASUNDER

Today is a happy summer holiday,
Surely, Shakespeare fell in love on a Summer day
and compared his love to the beauty of summer.

MISS BEATRICE

You are right. In his sonnet,
"Shall I compare thee to a summer's day?"

MISS ASUNDER

I wish I could be his mistress,
I'll call him my Tchinda Shakespeare!
But I am worn-out by distress

MISS BEATRICE

Summer is the lovers' season.
Even squirrels go out in twos for a reason.

MISS ASUNDER

What of those that go out in ones?

MISS BEATRICE

They return in twos; they'd once
Been ones also, remember?

MISS ASUNDER

Only fortunate twos have once been ones.

MISS BEATRICE

Cast your net in the right place,
Use the right bait to displace and outpace,
Anyone, remember, no coup de grace!
We must be ready to win even to efface!

MISS ASUNDER

I'm famished; I haven't cooked awhile
Let's go to the restaurant and dine.
What was he doing home when you left?
He turned down my invitation so deaf!
My heart is sinking and sicken bereft!

MISS BEATRICE

He was writing another book *Miss Seraphim:* The Evil Behind the Law.

MISS ASUNDER

Well—he should be a lawyer!
Since he is a man who loves to be loyal.

MISS BEATRICE

I kind of think so—too!

MISS ASUNDER

I will get him a nice Cameroonian dish,
A surprise for his birthday. What does he like best, or what can be his wish?

MISS BEATRICE

He likes achu and corn fufu.
He is a native of Baligham—grew up
In Bamenda and Mbouda, as a grown-up,
He attended the University of Dschang.

MISS ASUNDER

Does he love corn fufu?
Feeding a man's heart is through his stomach. That could be a bait to ransom my love.

MISS BEATRICE

A man's stomach is through his heart!
Food can sometimes help to kickstart,
A man's love and interest for a woman

MISS ASUNDER

What of my love counterpart?

MISS BEATRICE

She's African and good at it all,
She can cook, to have a man fall,
She twerks to have a man tremble
Victory is ours if we don't fumble.

MISS ASUNDER

Wretched of a woman, I am!
I grew up with a cook,
Now I can't cook; I am a crook!
I can twerk, squish and even squirt,
Here I am, wretched of a woman!

MISS BEATRICE

You must beat Miss Angel.
She can cook achu, eru, Joll of rice

MISS ASUNDER

How fairy is she?

MISS BEATRICE

She's below fairy,
She's hairy!

MISS ASUNDER

I might need a chef!
If not—I am doomed!
I see it so apparent the gloom.

MISS BEATRICE

Cheer up—
He will be your groom!
You will one day together jump the broom

MISS ASUNDER

Miss Angel,
Do you think he loves her?

MISS BEATRICE

Aren't you the choice of all men?
I see nothing yet, nothing omen!
He's still yours at this moment!

MISS ASUNDER

Is she of noble feminist blood and law too?

MISS BEATRICE

Not a feminist noble blood by birth,
She became one through the law after birth.

Miss Beatrice and Miss Asunder finally get to the restaurant.

EXIT

ACT 3—SCENE 1

NARRATOR

(Off Stage)

A master of the craft, William Shakespeare,
So well-known for his heavy wit so clear,
"If music be the food of love, play on,"
In his famous play "Twelfth Night."
Love is to the heart, as music to the soul adheres,
A good blend for lovers' hearts in good gear.
When dark comes, when stars shine at night,
Love becomes a pleasant ride, all right or alright.
Of this noble place in the city—Times Square,
Is where our lovers have chosen with delight
To quench the anxiety of this aflame love despite,
All oaths and caprices against them or in spite
Of all the subtilties of Beatrice and Asunder!
Now let me tell you what I see and foresee,
So long of a car, pretty like a bridal's train,
Therein is a compatible pair, love adorn in wonder!
So compatible, so gentle in their steps, in fact, infallible.
City music grows so wild, as people wander in wonder,
What an admirable, adorable love so insatiable.

Love is a baby; it may happen but must be trained,
There's no true love as true as what you make perfect,

Love is a shapeless clay in the hands of two fallible lovers,
Who either decide to make it perfect and correct
Or let things go wrong in all aspects in neglect.
Every true love story had once been a project,
Love isn't a ready-made dress that you put on or expect
To be so blissful, always infallibly romantic in effect.
We all have feelings, desires that sometimes don't intersect,
Here comes the nightmare, lack of respect or introspect,
Here comes the dread, when we become capricious suspects,
When our selfish desires are not met or willfully subject,
To one another's care, preference, our ego becomes deject.

True love begins from within; let's all retrospect,
Our greatest enemy lies within us; let's reflect
Love isn't happiness when you bring nothing to the table,
Love is a choice, sometimes a feeling so insatiable or unstable
If one's desire isn't tamed, it can lead to a conflict,
The end of some love tales are easy to predict,
This is my impression, not a verdict,
Let's watch what happens if it does contradict
What I think is of love, as Saint Benedict.

INT. RESTAURANT - TIMES SQUARE - DAY

Music is playing. Fireworks are all over the place in Times Square, New York City. The restaurant is not too crowded. Miss Beatrice and Miss Asunder request seats at the restaurant's VIP section. Hours later, a limousine pulls by the restaurant's glass door. The door opens. All restaurant eyes are anxious to see the VIP who will come out of the limousine. Miss Angel and Mr. Tchinda enter.

MISS ASUNDER

Have they been together in time past,
For Tchinda to give in to her so fast?

MISS BEATRICE

Worry not of their past
Be brave, don't be downcast.
I know very little of her past—that outcast
Until when she became on him an enthusiast.

MISS ASUNDER

She might have bewitched him,
I hear Africans are good at magic.
She might have used a magic wand to whim
His mind off me to respond so automatic.

MISS BEATRICE

Beauty and money is the only magic
We'll push them to their limit-elastic
Their love will fall apart so dramatic.
Every man has a flaw his soft spot or panic
Button. Once pressed, all will be realistic.

Mr. Tchinda and Miss Angel enter the same restaurant arm in arm in Times Square, New York. The crowd is yelling out of excitement to see the famous poet and playwright. Mr. Tchinda notices that Miss Beatrice and Miss Asunder are seated in the restaurant's VIP section. With arm locked with Miss Angel, they both walk in that direction.

MR. TCHINDA

Bon appétit, mes dames !

MISS ASUNDER

What a surprise—so romantic?
Exquisite gentleman and acrobatic.

Suddenly, Miss Asunder begins to blush uncontrollably. She grabs a paper napkin on the table and tries to clean her face. Uneasy with Tchinda and Miss Angel's presence, she gives Tchinda a hug, followed by a handshake to Miss Angel. Miss Beatrice is silent, staring at both Miss Angel and Tchinda.

MISS ASUNDER

I reserved a seat for you here.
Drink as much wine or even beer
To my bill, if you want to dare
Drink to stupor, let your spirit stir.

Anxious in her mind, she tries to offer the closest seat by her left-hand side, where Tchinda will sit in between Miss Angel and Miss Asunder. Miss Angel will be directly sitting opposite Miss Beatrice while she can sit and lean on Tchinda's body.

MR. TCHINDA

Thanks a million for your generosity
We prefer somewhere else, with luminosity.

MISS ASUNDER

I can offer you a better place with sumptuosity,

Please, don't turn down my grandiosity,
At least for once, in reciprocity.

MR. TCHINDA

Such a moment is so unfateful,
However, please, Angel, meet Asunder.
Asunder, here's miss Angel, my angel.

MISS ANGEL

I am so delighted to meet you, Asunder!

MISS ASUNDER

My deadly rival in the same den!
The one he has been seeing now and then!
Can I revenge? How and when?

(boiling with anger within)

Mr. JAMES enters the restaurant. The attendant leads Miss Angel and Mr. Tchinda to another VIP table directly opposite the one where Miss Asunder and Miss Beatrice are sitting. On the table is written RESERVED for Miss Angel and Tchinda.

MISS ASUNDER

(to Beatrice)

Is she—she?

MISS BEATRICE

Yes, she is the she.

MISS ASUNDER

What's her parentage?

MISS BEATRICE

Sorry, did you say percentage?

MISS ASUNDER

Not—Parentage!

MISS BEATRICE

She's from a pauper peasant family.
Not still sure how she came to America,
Her parent must have sold all their lands,
And even the entire village, or Africa,
To get a flight ticket to this wonderland.
She's such a filthy rag, so ugly and clammy.

MISS ASUNDER

Where they this wretched?

MISS BEATRICE

She looks like French bread,
It was all they could afford instead
Of eating healthy or a balanced diet.
She's very sneaky, where she's so quiet.

Mr. Tchinda and Miss Angel sit at the other table.

MISS ANGEL

Who was that lady?
She seems of a type shabby and shady!
Appearing friendly but very deadly.

MR. TCHINDA

She's a snare!
She pretends to care,
As you said, beware!

MISS ANGEL

Women of such are everywhere,
We know them; they're aware
When they visit a place or go somewhere,
They want everyone to know they own the air
They stand tall, above everyone to compare.

MR. TCHINDA

Things of such nowadays are not rare,
They spend time fashioning their hair,
And to give attention to their soiree wear.
Let them mind their business; who cares?

MISS ANGEL

Isn't she the one in the house you live?
Her face looks unhappy and pale,
The moment we got in, she's not vive.

MR. TCHINDA

She has joined the club of glamor!
She has been entangled and trapped in lust,

She's so lost, sometimes we clamor,
When she wants me in their game, intrust.

MISS ANGEL

What's her relationship with Asunder?
Such friendship makes me wonder,
If truly it's genuine, there's something under.
Have you thought of it too or ponder?

MR. TCHINDA

Of course, I have pondered,
Their secrets are kept under
Anyone daring to follow them will blunder.

MISS ANGEL

What's the secret under?
Did they kill or plunder?

MR. TCHINDA

I was told by Beatrice the night I came.
One unfortunate mourning warning morning
She was driven to school in her usual glamour.
She loved music, sang for attraction and valor.
As a pet dog of the family, one and only daughter
She possessed all that could give her laughter.
Her parents were wealthy and were her provider
She lived a life of affluence and influence.
Her parents traveled in their private flight
It was their routine; she bragged with delight.
She was friends with everyone for money,
But wasn't friendly with anyone, not of her class.

She lived in a castle, only with her caste.
The news came to her without mercy,
A plane crashed, and her parents had died,
In a mountainous area, so broad and vast.
She'd cried, but no one cared except Beatrice,
She was still of a noble heart like Fabrice
Until the demon, Judas Iscariot, got hold of her.
Asunder inherited great fortunes from her parents,
She starved for love and was often stabbed by love
She'd fallen in love by her alluring beauty
For beauty and wealth, men came as lovers
But they were all robbers and rovers.
Beatrice, who was her classmate,
Became her intimate mate,
Consoling her to await for her soulmate,
Time was never too late.
The rest is history-

MISS ANGEL

I perceive there is trouble—she is!

MR. TCHINDA

She's not my taste nor shoe size,
I feel her pain and her parent's demise,
Rich people always think they know all,
Because of money, they tend to despise advice,
Even when see the blunder or about to fall.

MISS ANGEL

Well—she needs someone for real advice
Though rich and pretty, they're all disguise,

Deep within her, she knows a void lies!

MR. TCHINDA

It's unfortunate, we can't do otherwise!

Miss Asunder and Miss Beatrice have just finished eating. Miss Asunder calls the restaurant attendant. She cannot help herself from not looking at Tchinda and Miss Angel at their table.

MISS ASUNDER

Please, how much is my bill?

MR. JAMES

One thousand dollars.

MISS ASUNDER

What about the bill of the gentleman sitting with
that lady?

They whisper in a low voice, not to attract Tchinda or Miss Angel's attention.

MR. JAMES

Two thousand.

MISS ASUNDER

That's four thousand dollars.
Keep the rest or the change!
Here is my card, please keep close range,
Let me know of anything so strange

She then gives her business card to Mr. James.

MR. JAMES

Thank you, Madam!

(exit)

Miss Asunder and her friend are done eating. They stand up to depart. Miss Asunder walks closer to the table where Miss Angel and Tchinda are sitting. She comes and stands directly behind Tchinda, running her left hand on his head provocatively.

MISS ASUNDER

We're on our way to the house
I am going to my jailhouse!

MR. TCHINDA

Drive safe!

MISS ASUNDER

(to Angel)

What did you say was your name?

MISS ANGEL

Angel.

MISS ASUNDER

Angel or Angel?

MISS ANGEL

Miss Angel.

MISS ASUNDER

Now I know for sure!
The one who makes me to endure.
Tchinda, please give a ring tonight.
My poet and famous playwright.

Miss Asunder and Miss Beatrice now exit the restaurant.

MISS ANGEL

Do you owe her a ring?

MR. TCHINDA

No, I don't.

MISS ANGEL

Yes, she said so.

MR. TCHINDA

Yes, she said so,
But never meant so!

MISS ANGEL

What then did she mean by that?

MR. TCHINDA

She meant a call.

MISS ANGEL

The English language is confuzzling.

MR. TCHINDA

We speak languages,
But don't understand languages.

MISS ANGEL

That's spoonerism!
Let's pay and get out of here.

MR. TCHINDA

Yes, my angel.
Thanks for the birthday retreat.

MISS ANGEL

Waiter, come, please!

MR. TCHINDA

How much is my bill?

Mr. James re-enters the restaurant.

MR. JAMES

Sorry, sir!
Did you say your bee?

MR. TCHINDA

Bill and not bee.

MR. JAMES

Sorry, sir.
The lady who left paid for you all.
Here is your receipt, thanks for coming!
(stretching out the receipt)

MR. TCHINDA

(confuzzled)

Did she?

MR. JAMES

Yes, sir.
I believe you must be a lucky gentleman.

MR. TCHINDA

Thanks. It's okay!

MISS ANGEL

The battle has just begun!

EXIT

ACT 3—SCENE 2

INT. TELEPHONIC CONVERSATION - 11:00 PM

That same evening, after returning from the restaurant, Miss Beatrice and Miss Asunder, in a phone call, plot Miss Angel's downfall to get her fired from her job. She is the main obstacle that has been preventing Mr. Tchinda from paying Miss Asunder's attention.

MISS ASUNDER

Tchinda, is such a hard nut to crack.
Does he sometimes smoke crack?

MISS BEATRICE

He's just a little naïve and arrogant brat,
We'll crush him, like a little rat
He will no choice but to fallback,
He won't only fallback but fall flat.

MISS ASUNDER

Is he back?

MISS BEATRICE

No, I have not heard him bark,
I won't give my eyes sleep till he's back,
But once back, then I begin my attack.

MISS ASUNDER

Well said,
Perhaps he needs some wrath,
To know that life is a rough path.
Let's make him go through a glide path,
For him, know and feel the terror of bloodbath.
Since has decided to venture on a warpath.

MISS ASUNDER

A stone used to crack palm nut
Either cracks the nut or the nut
Cracks the stone.

MISS BEATRICE

I am the stone; he's the calabash!
Whether the stone first hits the calabash,
Or the calabash first hits the stone,
The calabash must crack

MISS ASUNDER

While you deal with him on your side,
I will deal with Angel by her side.
I now know where she works,
I will reduce to nothing but a corpse.
Some men are like dogs,
Once you give them bones to eat,
You can make them your watchdogs,
Or you can make them leapfrogs,
To obey you without error and speed.

MISS BEATRICE

Great!
Then the game is easy to play.
Once both have been preyed,
They will know, some women are highways,
When you see them drive on beltways,
Don't obstruct their path; give them a freeway.

MISS ASUNDER

Tchinda, I love you,
But you're biting more than you can chew,
You now make my love a foolish shew,
Because of a brat—ugly as a shrew.
I will crush her; then she'll know I am true,
The woman that you can't face or go through,
Watch, wait, and see me come through,
Watch, wait, and see me cut through,
Watch, wait, and see me get through,
Watch, wait, and see me breakthrough,
Watch, wait, and see me act like a corkscrew,
Before your eyes, you'll see him screwed!
Before his eyes, he'll see you screwed!

MISS BEATRICE

He has bitten more than he can swallow,
He will certainly come back or stoop low,
To beg for water even from his enemy,
To push it down his throat as the only remedy.

MISS ASUNDER

Is he finally back,
Or did you hear him bark?

MISS BEATRICE

Nothing as of yet, but I see clouds,
I am the clouds, don't have any doubts,
That it will rain on him so hot and hard.
Tonight will be his D-day or graveyard.
I am well stationed; I am at the vanguard
Waiting for him, I must give him a red card.

MISS ASUNDER

A friend in need is a friend indeed,
You make me proud of your good deed.
A noble Cameroonian, a rare breed.

MISS BEATRICE

Peace! Peace!
I will weed out the bad weed!
I will trample upon him as in a stampede.
Before I am done with him, he must cede
I am of good hope; we will succeed,
To break him down, then weed out his conceit.
I have the knife well sharpened, and the yam
Once done, he thinks he'd been in a traffic jam.

MISS ASUNDER

I am all consumed by love and rage,
Until I get him or take revenge,

My life is nothing but a shadow,
Nobody dares me without getting an elbow!

MISS BEATRICE

Snow does not fall only on one roof.
He will soon know he erred once disproved.
The pot that cooks food most scrumptious,
Is always not given credit or seen suspicious.
We'll get him or them, by other mean officious,
No matter how it seems now, inauspicious.
Sleep in peace, in your mansion avaricious,
Victory is ours; it's not any suppositious.
He is naïve to see angel's love flagitious.

MISS ASUNDER

Love is a songbook written in lyrics,
Some in chapters and choruses,
While other chapters are in despair and sorrows.

MISS BEATRICE

When crickets cry at midnight,
There is a change of season ahead.
A warning sign, before dusk or daylight.
Only deaf ears will regret, shrink or shred.
Chattering birds never build a good nest
For themselves; give yourself some rest.
Call angel's manager, put him to test?

MISS ASUNDER

I will do so tonight,
Before I give my eyes rest.

End of phone conversation between Miss Beatrice and Miss Asunder. Miss Asunder is consumed in her thoughts after the call. Desperately talking to herself, she moves aimlessly from one corner of her living room to the other, wondering what allegations to bring against Miss Angel.

MISS ASUNDER

(soliloquy)

I must look for angel's flaw
That will lead to her downfall.
Her job, her only anchor and hope
Without which, she can't cope.
If she can be fired, she will be down
She'll be hard-pressed, in her bill will drown
I must revenge, she must come to her knees,
Then kiss my ass if she ever wants peace…

EXIT

ACT 3—SCENE 3

NARRATOR

(Off Stage)

If you love me, don't touch me until you tell me so,
If you tell me so and don't love me, don't touch me.
All I need is love, but prefer it slow in the snow,
To hug, hold, and kiss you when it's really cold.

If you love me, don't touch me; if you do,
Make me feel special, moan, groan, and aglow,
And I will be yours forever and will let them know
How much I cherish you till we grow old.
I'll feed you with wild honey, give you my chateau,
I'll tell you ancient tales and put on your best bandeau.

My two virgin lilies are there fresh and idle on my torso,
Make of it what you want, a feeding bottle or pillow,
If you choose to instead call me Juliet, I will call you Romeo,
Let of this love be so genuine, not a quid pro quo,
Nothing do I desire in return, except you I desire.
Once love is kindled, it burns as a savage wildfire.

If you don't love me,
Don't touch me; if you do, let it be forever,
That you'll give it to me, whenever and wherever,

I'll make you a garland, and crown you my king,
The king of my heart, to rule over my body whichever
You want, however, and whatsoever you want.

If you don't love me,
Don't touch me; if you do, let me be yours,
So that we write our love history together
In your arms, let me be colored, but love assured,
All I need is to feel you in all odds weather.
Seasons will go by; strangers by, but altogether
We shall be one to fight for our love, not to wither.

I'm ready to learn from you, be my UNESCO.
If love is a school, each me higher and higher,
If love is a poem, teach me stylistic devices, satire,
If love is a flower, give me one that lives forever,
If love is sacrilege, yours is instead a privilege!

INT. HARLEM CENTRAL PARK - MORNING

Tchinda spends the night with Miss Angel in her apartment after his birthday. Both lovers have decided to spend another day together. Mr. Tchinda's right hand is crossed over Miss Angel's shoulder as they walk around the beautiful man-made lake of Harlem Central Park, New York City.

MISS ANGEL

I see smoke from afar,
This's an omen of strange fire,
Asunder's strange feeling or desire.

MR. TCHINDA

You can kill two lovers, never their love.
We all born, bred, and bonded by fate,
Nothing can stand our way, not even hate
From Asunder's treacherous abate!
I know she's evil, nothing more to debate,
But she needs repentance for a breastplate.

MISS ANGEL

You're the best melody of all to sing,
Your voice sounds like a guitar string.
Look at the fish from this lake?
They know I am love consumed and razed,
Your love is the only thing I can graze,
You've set me on fire, so hot ablaze,
What else can I ask you, money or honey?
Please, kiss me; I am hot and horny,
Hug me hard against your chest,
Let's play hide and see or chess.

MR. TCHINDA

(poesy oration)

She Felt She Fell in Love

I waited for a bus by the roadside.
With the flute of my lips, I sang a new song.
She stood by me, a lady, and then she did sigh.
Her features were pretty and strong.
But the reason she sighed I didn't know.
Maybe she thought she was growing old.
She asked, "Are you a singer?"

But I heard, "Are you still single?"
Maybe sighed because she was single,
Wanting to mingle,
But a ring on her finger

I did see; I guessed a ring of marriage.
Maybe she thought marriage was love,
But later, I saw that love is marriage.
Could it be, with me, she fell and felt in love?
Or she was falling and feeling in love with my new song?

Sooner her bus came by, and there she was gone.
All I knew was that she had a problem,
But I hope it was not on me her blame
Of being lovesick and sick of love.
I wished I had told her I was single and a singer
To sing to heart some of my poems in lyrics
And to take her into my arms as a single singer.

For her to sing my chorus
And to banish her sorrows
If I sang her a love song, and she also sang
To me, it's chorus; we would have both fallen and felt in love.
She would have been happy.
I would have been happy.
And we could later marry and be merry.

MISS ANGEL

Asunder, hope certainly not,
I know she's crazy and nut.

MR. TCHINDA

(poesy oration)

The Witness of My Weakness

I have seen something in life,
All human efforts and desires
Are like hidden two-edged swords.
All is vanity upon vanity.

Some toil and moil for pleasure,
Others weary wildly for leisure,
Yet still grow and go old
Without still the gold.

This true and only pure gold
Is not in the heights.
Neither is it in the depths.
What somebody calls weakness
Is to me a witness.

Please, a minute, wait,
This is something I have
Just received.
Young boys and men,
Listen to this.

Never say, "I need a perfect wife."
The weaknesses of every wife
Is a wise man's wisdom and strength.

Let us debate awhile.
If a wise man sees a gold deposit,
Won't he dig deeper and deeper?

If a wise midwife sees a gold deposit,
Won't he not dig the womb
Of the earth to discover
This amazing pregnancy?

Young girls, women,
Never say, "I need a perfect man."
Let us again debate.

In the beginning were perfect men,
These perfect men were with a perfect Man,
And this perfect Man
Was in these perfect men,
And these men were perfect
Until Eve came.

You are very right to say
I need a perfect man,
But let us have a closer debate.
To ask for a perfect man
Means you are a perfect woman.
If then you are already a perfect woman,
If what you need now is a perfect man,
Why then again talk of perfection?

This, I will explicate.
Don't you know your weakness
And his weakness
All bear you witness
To your imperfection and perfection?
If no, why should iron sharpen iron?

I am not a man.
So I speak not for men.
I am not a woman.
So I speak not for women,
But when a man and a woman
Become mates and mate,
They all create and procreate.
This is the simple process I mean.
A woman from a man receives
She becomes pregnant or conceives
And is later delivered of a child.

What you conceive,
Of it, you become pregnant.
And of what you are pregnant of,
You also are delivered of.
As a man thinks,
So is he.

MISS ANGEL

(Singing)

J'ai toujours rêvé te dire ceci un jour. C'est depuis, ce jour, que je vis le jour, Le jour où je fis ta connaissance Et l'amour eu sa naissance.

MR. TCHINDA

(Poesy Oration)

Ma charmante chair chère chérie,
Tu deviens une poétesse,
L'amour est une noblesse,
Mais la joie d'aimer est dans nos faiblesses, Même

si dans nos faiblesses, On se blesse.
C'est là ou Dieu veut qu'on découvre sa richesse.
L'amour est un don de Grace, à toute race,
Pour rendre grâce a son Créateur.

MISS ANGEL

Amen!

EXIT

ACT 3—SCENE 4

EXT. NEW YORK CITY - EVENING

Later that evening, Miss Asunder and Mr. Tchinda return back to the same eatery. Sooner they get into the restaurant, a teenage boy runs in for help.

TEENAGER

(entering restaurant)

Excuse me, sir!
Where is the restroom?

MR. TCHINDA

This is a cafeteria.
Restrooms are found in a hotel.

MR. JAMES

(entering)

Do you need help, sir?

TEENAGER

Yes, sir!
Where is the restroom?

MR. JAMES

(pointing to the restroom)

That way, sir.

MR. TCHINDA

Excuse me, sir!
Was he asking for the resting room?

MR. JAMES:

No, sir!
Not the resting room—the toilets.

MR. TCHINDA

I heard him say resting room.
Why not just say toilet?

MR. JAMES

He didn't say so, sir!
He said restroom.

MR. TCHINDA

Do you also have hotels
Herewith resting rooms?

MR. JAMES

(exiting)

No, we don't. He meant toilets.

MISS ANGEL

Bae, let it go!
That's how they call it.
Let's get something and eat.

(Exit James)
MR. TCHINDA

I've already eaten.

MISS. ANGEL

When,
We've been together all through,
I didn't see you eat nor chew!
Isn't it true?

MR. TCHINDA

You're right,
I have been eaten by your love
I have been bitten by your love,
I have been beaten by your love,
I have been smitten by your love,
I have been smidgen by your love.
What else do I need to eat to satiety?

Mr. James re-enters with a bottle of water and a glass on the tray for Tchinda.

MISS. ANGEL

You might have been eaten by my love,
You might have been bitten by my love,
You might have been beaten by my love,

You might have been smitten by my love,
You might have been smidgen by my love,
But one thing remains undone,
One stone remains unturned!

MR. TCHINDA

What's it?

MISS. ANGEL

You need to eat real food!
Love is to the heart, as food is to stomach!
(Re-enter James to take their order)

MR. JAMES

Excuse me, sir!
Can I please get your order?

MISS. ANGEL

Can we some achu and some soya?

MR. JAMES

(Turning to Tchinda)

What about you, sir!

MR. TCHINDA

Our likes are alike!

MR. JAMES

If I may ask, sir, are you English?

MR. TCHINDA

Yes, I speak English.

MR. JAMES

No, sir. I didn't say English.
I was asking you if you are British.

MR. TCHINDA

Can you rephrase your phrase?
Did you say brutish?

MR. JAMES

No, sir. I didn't say brutish.
I said British, from England.

MR. TCHINDA

Sorry, sir!
For that linguistic malapropism.
I did not become British by birth,
But after imperial colonization and rebirth.
And were forced to learn imperial pragmatism.

MR. JAMES

You have a French accent,
Impact of British and French
Colonial rule, right?

MR. TCHINDA

Well—kind of sort!
Cameroon became a class *B mandate*
under the League of Nations.
On July 20, 1922, Kamerun was split
and given to Britain and France.
By December 13, 1946, it became
a United Nations' Trust Territory.

MR. JAMES

Are you English or French?

MR. TCHINDA

Both!
Some are Anglophones.

MISS. ANGEL

Bae, I am hungry, let him go!

MR. JAMES

Sorry, madame!
I will be back with your order.
(Exit James)

MISS ANGEL

Behind every language is a culture.

MR. TCHINDA

You're right; that's why Cameroon

And Canada is the only two bilingual
English and French-speaking nations—

MISS ANGEL

Bilingual on papers!

MR. TCHINDA

The evil of colonial colonization.
We're now colonial marionettes
Who have been brainwashed into civilization,
Another form of white annexation.
We've so much embraced, even the internet,
That we're now slaves, tossed around as pets.

MISS ANGEL

Well—
The Beautiful Ones Are Not Yet Born

MR. TCHINDA

Some are already born
But needs to be born again or reborn.
(Re-enter James with the food)

MR. JAMES

Here in America,
You might have an accent issue?

MISS ANGEL

Please, let me get more tissue!

MR. JAMES

(continues)

You need to take some ESL lessons
(i.e., English as a second language).

MR. TCHINDA

America is a linguistic melting pot
My accent adds diversity worth support,
A linguistic pride of this culturaliness,
What else brings America happiness?
Is it not because we speak Englishes?

MR. JAMES

Englishes, you are right,
Many may not be alight.

MR. TCHINDA

They don't need to be all right!

MISS ANGEL

Should all be assimilated into
American English?

MR. TCHINDA

What then is the pride of diversity?
To attend college or university?
To be accepted in the city of the universe?

MR. JAMES

Well—it's subjective,

We're in together irrespective
Of our differences or prospective.
(Exit James)

MISS ANGEL

I feel the fire burning,
I see it burning so vicious!

MR. TCHINDA

Let it burn!
Not all vicious fire that burns consumes!

EXIT

ACT 3—SCENE 5

INT. MISS BEATRICE'S APARTMENT - 9:00 PM

Mr. Tchinda and Miss Angel part ways after the restaurant, as Mr. Tchinda returns to Miss Beatrice's apartment.

MISS BEATRICE

Here you're alas!
Where have you been in days past?

MR. TCHINDA

Where else can I be?
I've been busy as a bee!

MISS BEATRICE

Busy as a bee, you say?

MR. TCHINDA

Aren't bees always busy,
Would you have preferred, dizzy?

MISS BEATRICE

Busy or dizzy won't make it easy,
Let's not waste time on things flimsy!

MR. TCHINDA

Time wasted to me is clumsy!
What's at stake, something queasy!

MISS BEATRICE

Something quizzy,
If you care, call it queasy or fuzzy!

MR. TCHINDA

Then, squeeze the quiz!

MISS BEATRICE

Have you made up your mind?

MR. TCHINDA

My mind has always been made up,
It can't be made down.

MISS BEATRICE

Only a stubborn fly
Follows a corpse to the grave,
That's is something very grave.

MR. TCHINDA

Only cowards fear to brave the grave,
Because they're coward, never brave!

MISS BEATRICE

Did you call me a coward?

MR. TCHINDA

I said cowards,
I didn't say you, are you?

MISS BEATRICE

My wrath will make you rot?

MR. TCHINDA

Is your wrath a rod?

MISS BEATRICE

I will call 911 if you dare a word?

MR. TCHINDA

Of course, 911 is for cowards,
Must every issue involve 911?
What if you instead tried dialing 119?

MISS BEATRICE

My wrath is getting venomous!
Hold your tongue before something heinous.

MR. TCHINDA

How venomous is your venom enormous?

MISS BEATRICE

(Getting her phone to dial 911)

MR. TCHINDA

(continues)

Your face glows, rather than blush,
Are you perchance not being rushed,
By your sinful desires, so addictive or lushed?
You were once just, what erred with the trust?
That your heart is aflame with ardent lust,
You behave in a way, so vilest to entrust,
A way might seem right, but it leads to rust,
If care is not taken, or your heart flushed,
From these misdeeds, you will be crushed.
You can bring the devil in you, in disgust.
Time is our reward for good or evil deeds.

Out of anger and guilt, Miss Beatrice slaps Tchinda, hoping he will fight back in return for her to have a case to build against him.

MR. TCHINDA

A Cameroonian, more American than Americans?

MISS BEATRICE

You're a disgrace to African hood!
A misfit in this neighborhood.
In you is nothing, I mean nothing good!
You've marred your way to manhood,
You've chosen pains than life in leisure,
You've chosen love in place of pleasure,
I am sure she bewitch you into her womanhood

MR. TCHINDA

No amount of snowfall on a black
Will wash him white in America.
While we are here, always have a flashback
That you're in America, but came from Africa!
You can be American on paper,
But your skin color is still a shaper,
That defines your joy or destiny.
Don't forget the contrast or irony,
We're all equal, but our hearts separate

MISS BEATRICE

Have you become a racist?

MRS. FABRICE

Not a racist, a classicist!

MISS BEATRICE

When you go to Rome,
Do what the Romans do.

MR. TCHINDA

The Romans are to Rome
Cameroonians are to Cameroon.
America for Americans,
So is Miss Angel to Tchinda.

MISS BEATRICE

You've abused my trust and generosity
Either in naivety, loquacity, or curiosity,

I have decided, based on your monstrosity
That we must part ways, starting today,
Get your stuff, leave without any delay!

MR. TCHINDA

Our ways have long parted,
Since your love for me became so corrupt,
My heart also had long departed
I knew the battle has just started.
I'm not taken abashed or so abrupt,
I still love you and of your generosity past,
None of these deeds have been discarded,
Though our love is cold, now deserted.
It's sad and pathetic, but again cathectic,
That we depart on such a note so chaotic.
We're of the same class and caste,
But no love for one another—so steadfast
To what is evil and what we see others do.
I am not your enemy, nor an iconoclast,
We must learn to build enduring love that last!
Adieu!

MISS BEATRICE

Enough of that folly,
Don't camouflage your Polly!
You've brought me nothing but melancholy
Now, you recite venomous poetry so unholy?
I am dialing 911 now, if you don't haste!

MR. TCHINDA

Don't anchor evil on 911,
They're neither the anchor of evil,
Though we've made them look so.

EXIT

ACT 4—SCENE 1

NARRATOR

(Off Stage)

It's so unfortunate; there isn't any school so unique,
There's no subject to study every midweek,
It's all a universe of its own, sometimes bleak!
Everyone can be preyed on, rich, poor, strong, or weak.
Sometimes what we feel, and think is love we seek,
Is nothing but a wrong feeling driving you sick.
It's difficult to say what is love's preference, our physique?
Love and beauty bring delight to the heart, so to speak,
But the heart is deceitful, evil as said a mystique.
There's a law of love and attraction that make lovers click,
This law is natural, not a man-made technique.
Somethings we pray for to come in haste or quick,
Others we get ready for; once it comes, it's not oblique.
What is divinely put together is always and forever click,
Like Odysseus and Penelope, or Orpheus and Eurydice!
Not every lover who comes together were meant to clique.
Love that is and will be sometimes begin so unusual,
Nothing can be done about it; it's mutual and visual.
Some friends are only good for a relationship commutual,
When friendship and love become a toss, boss, or pari-mutuel,
And the grounds to love or justify why we must fall in love,

We're in serious error, erring in delusion, and the rest of,
It like Miss Asunder's tale who refuses to let go of,
What never belonged to her in her destitute attempts of
Getting Tchinda sold to Miss Angel's love, he can't get rid of.

I understand Asunder's misconception of love or chagrin,
Though pretty and wealthy, she thinks she can break-in,
That is, in every man's heart, or even foreskin.
To get her way through her vicious paradise built-in.
She fails to see in Tchinda; there is a godly man within him,
A virtuous man, not a wolf in sheepskin,
Who's lust free of her captive beauty, moral and mortal sin.
Love is beyond just the pleasures underneath or within
Our mortal flesh, with which we're clothes herein.
Some have erred so in thoughts and argument,
What else can a pretty lady do to trap or underpin,
A man's heart for herself, or kindle the love that has been
Apart from her treacherous and feminist armament?

I do so love her, but sometimes she's too impetuous,
When the signs are there, clear and perspicuous.
She is a mistress of misdeeds, unconspicuous or iniquitous
Who will dread not daring the great Mount Olympus,
The mount of the gods, sacred for the clean of hearts.
Let me hold my tranquility, and let's see how she's smart
She's beautifully pretty, of course, isn't it just an art?
Let daring devils continue to dare,
Let her continue her play; I will continue to play my part!

INT. MISS ASUNDER'S MANSION – EVENING

Mr. Tchinda has been sent out from Miss Beatrice's house. On his way to meet his only hope, Miss Angel, he stops in Miss Asunder's mansion. Tchinda then knocks at the door and enters.

MISS. ASUNDER

Alas!
My long-awaited guest.
I am sure you came alone, I guess!

MR. TCHINDA

Alone, but not lonely!

MISS. ASUNDER

True!
You can't be lonely in my presence,
There is everything glowing luminescence
Just accept my love in its intumescence,
All I need is submission and your obeisance,
That I love you with defects and acceptance.

MR. TCHINDA

Are you now a drammarian?

MISS. ASUNDER

Not a grammarian!

MISS ASUNDER

Are we on the same acquiescence?

MR. TCHINDA

You're the vilest of devils I know!

MISS ASUNDER

Forget about what you know,
Let's care about you don't know.
You have this to your pleasure,
A house, cars, money, free sex
I'll give you raw with no latex,
Nothing will perturb your pleasure.
On a condition for you to say yes!

MR. TCHINDA

You're a devil of a kind,
Not only generous but very kind,
You've paid my bills without my consent.
Is that supposed to mean a present?

MISS ASUNDER

Never mind,
Nothing of great concern!
Just an act of love, I hope you didn't mind.
That I paid your bills without consent?

MR. TCHINDA

Should generosity not be probed,
I feel as though I'm robbed!

MISS ASUNDER

You aren't robbed,
You are instead rubbed.
Can I get the same favor in return?
Just a yes, to make me certain!

MR. TCHINDA

You don't need to be certain,
My deeds are so plain or uncertain!
To know we are incompatible pair
To have any form of a love affair.

MISS ASUNDER

Men like you are very rare,
Please, let my love for you be clear,
I have fallen in love and ensnared,
How else can I tell you or declare
This love that burns within with flare?

MR. TCHINDA

What the eyes can't admire,
My heart cannot desire!

(receiving an incoming text from Miss Beatrice to Miss Asunder)

Game over.
We'll soon take over!

MISS ASUNDER

Am I not admirable, lovable, and able?
What can Miss Angel do that I am unable?
Money, cars, or sex? What's so implausible?

MR. TCHINDA

Of course,
You are all-round-able and able.
Your beauty has even become a fable,
Your mansion is wonderful, full of marble,
One thing I want you to know is this,
Having you as a friend makes me pleased,
You have everything for a man's heart bliss,
Love is a dish; others have different taste,
One's taste is another's poison or dislike.
Get me now wrong; you're a wonderful,
Since the day of our meeting at the airport,
Your generosity caught my heart's ears or strike,
I just want to be very honest and respectful,
To avoid you any form of feeling so fretful.

MISS ASUNDER

I have fallen more after your oratory,
I have already so fallen deep in your poetry.
Every other thing that comes is an allegory,
That does not redeem me from this purgatory.
I'm at your mercy; redeem me from this lavatory.

MR. TCHINDA

It's such a sob story,
I feel your pain, so ambulatory,

I am also love consumed by someone's love.
We all have our love territory,
Your pain is woeful but still transitory.
Let's be friends, where there's no law mandatory

MISS ASUNDER

Your words break my heart's repository,
I have listened to you speak with auditory
I know so deep within, you're my remedy,
You're my remedy; you're my melody,
If loving you is a crime, let me accept it as a felony.
My heart is broken, what else to say, a threnody?

MR. TCHINDA

Courage is the greatest therapist,
Make it a priority on your list!
Let this sickened emotion die or decrease!

MISS ASUNDER

You're my only therapist,
I am love bound, waiting for your release!
Your love is like a lease,
I can't break without having a crease.

MR. TCHINDA

Maybe you need to see a priest!

MISS ASUNDER

You're my priest,
Who else can deliver me from this yeast?
A yeast, so strong as to also call a beast.

MR. TCHINDA

We all have our predicament!
Yours is love; mine is shelter.

MISS ASUNDER

Mine is beyond a predicament,
A chastisement—be my medicament,
And will also be your medicament.

MR. TCHINDA

My predicament is not an ailment,
That requires a form of medicament.

MISS ASUNDER

Why are you without abris?

MR. TCHINDA

My abris has become my debris!

MISS ASUNDER

Any crime of any degree?

MR. TCHINDA

None, neither of any degree or decree!

MISS ASUNDER

This doesn't speak well of her dignity.

MR. TCHINDA

Did I hear you say dignity—
Or you meant to say malignity?

MISS ASUNDER

I said dignity—

MR. TCHINDA

I never knew she had such an identity!
If you say so, then let it be so!

MISS ASUNDER

Aren't we of the same impression?

MR. TCHINDA

Yes,
We're in the same recession!
I have no further objection.

MISS ASUNDER

Let's spend the night here in reflection,
We can resolve this misconception.

MR. TCHINDA

I am strong to overcome rejection,
The rejected stone is the chief cornerstone!
Let me haste for a new dimension.

MISS ASUNDER

Outside is hostile and unfriendly night,
Don't venture into the night all alone,
Because of an altercation or dissention,
If you still want to dare, let me be your knight.
Let's ascend the secret dimension.
Let's together ease this love fire or tension.
Haste not into the night, there's apprehension

MR. TCHINDA

Together, we can't keep haste,
We don't have the pace or taste.
Farewell—

EXIT

ACT 4—SCENE 2

INT. MISS ASUNDER'S MANSION - LATE EVENING

Miss Asunder picks up her phone and dials some numbers. The phone rings the first time without anybody responding. Ten minutes later, she calls again and finally gets Mr. Martin, the museum manager who happens to be Miss Angel's manager.

MISS ASUNDER

(talking to Mr. Martin)

What have you been up to lately?
Anything hasty, tasty, daisy, or crazy?

MR. MARTIN

Nothing hazy, nor crazy!
Just reading, trying not to be lazy!

MISS ASUNDER

What are you reading?

MR. MARTIN

Tchinda's book. Our new Luther!

MISS ASUNDER

Martin Luther was a Baptist minister. Why do you think he was so successful in leading and driving change in America than other leaders and advocates?

MR. MARTIN

Martin Luther King had a different thinking paradigm … than his fellows

MISS ASUNDER

Horw?

MR. MARTIN

Luther had understood America's core value to mean *freedom, equality, and love. Not only did Christians need this freedom through salvation, but the society also* needed liberation from every form of oppression, beginning a *direct action* in Birmingham, Alabama.

MISS ASUNDER

Why did he resolve to direct action

Rather than following the path of peaceful Negotiation with the other eight clergymen?

MR. MARTIN

He that cannot be made to hear must be made to feel, as Luther justified his direct action in his letter, Letter from Birmingham City Jail. "… *We know through painful experience that freedom is never voluntarily given by the oppressor; it must be demanded by the oppressed…*"

MISS ASUNDER

Other civil rights activists had tried to break down racial barriers. Do you think Luther's success was a matter of luck, or because he was an elect?

MR. MARTIN

His success and credibility had nothing to do with being an elect, but his success was based on understanding divine timing and the people's need.

MISS ASUNDER

How can you justify that his action was divine timing and not just a success of chance or presumptuousness?

MR. MARTIN

Quoting from the horse's mouth,

"...For years now, I have heard the word wait!' It rings in the ear of every Negro with a piercing familiarity. This wait has almost always meant never. Justice too long delayed is justice denied. We have waited for more than 340 years for our constitutional and God-given rights..."

"Letter from Birmingham City Jail,

The Negro Is Your Brother" (April 16, 1963).

MISS ASUNDER

Well said, Martin.

I have waited for so long to fall in love

MR. MARTIN

(laughing over the telephone)

Fall in love? Love is a good thing.
If you fall, make sure you don't fall and remain on the ground.

MISS ASUNDER

I am not only on the ground,
But I am beneath or underground!
I am genuinely lost and confound!

MR. MARTIN

How can I unconfound you?

MISS ASUNDER

My fiancé
Snatched by one of your employees.
Which I want you to put her to her knees!

MR. MARTIN

It's somewhat ill-fated to hear this
What can I do for this pain to ease!

MISS ASUNDER

It might sound a satire,
But can you get her damn ass fired?
I don't care if she goes to hellfire!

MR. MARTIN

Who are we talking about?

MISS ASUNDER

She's called Angel!

MR. MARTIN

You know it is unfair.
For such personal issue or affair?

MISS ASUNDER

I just want to know she erred?
She bewitched him, for me to be in despair
She thinks she's so smart and blair,
But will crush and quash her like a bear!

MR. MARTIN

She's my assistant manager,
A woman known for her excellent morale
I am surprised to hear this immoral moral
Something strange, more to me a choral.

MISS ASUNDER

All that glitters is not gold,
She's perhaps good, but of a double fold,
Once at work, she acts very naïve and cold,
Once off duty, she keeps her morale on hold,
Then acts in a manner inappropriate or bold.

MR. MARTIN

I am still in doubt to hear this unfold,
Hearing it just from you, how can I uphold,
That such tale isn't a concocted stronghold?

MISS ASUNDER

I can get you an assistant manager,
Someone better in all qualities,

Someone with a better personality.
Not someone known for frivolity.
Like Angel—

MR. MARTIN

You sound bitter against her with hate,
That you desire her miserable or ablate.
I feel your pain, but difficult to relate,
To make her lose her job, or eliminate,
Why not look for another solution to this,
You must not wish her hell or the abyss.

MISS ASUNDER

Martin,
Let's strike a deal,
If you accept to bruise her heel,
You have your reward, in-kind or cash!
But you must have well smashed.

MR. MARTIN

Can we clearly define the terms,
For me to know what I get in returns?

MISS ASUNDER

Ten thousand in cash,
Free access to my kingdom,
Twice or thrice a day or night?
For one month.

MR. MARTIN

No bonus?

MISS ASUNDER

If well done, there's a bonus,
I will even feed you with wild locust!
If you don't mind, comer, let's sleepover!

They are laughing together.

END OF PHONE CALL

ACT 4—SCENE 3

INT. MISS ANGEL'S APARTMENT - 12:00 AM

Tchinda enters. Miss Angel, who is in her nightgown, is weeping on her love seat. Clouds are building up conspiracy in heaven, announcing the coming of rain.

MR. TCHINDA

You're chagrined!
What makes your heart bleats and bleeds,
As if the world was torn into bits?
Your face is pale, robbed of its grinned,
Nothing looks pleasant; even the air is thin.
Please, help me get some comprehension,
To lessen this unfiltered air or hypertension

MISS ANGEL

When the heart is chagrined,
Aren't the cracks seen on the face?
My heart is broken like a vase,
And my joy melting like ice within.

MR. TCHINDA

Stop sobbing and be not in this weep
Your tears lash my heart like a bitter whip,
Please, don't let your heart troubled or sink,

I am here for you, ready to melody or sing.

MISS ANGEL

For no reason so ideal to man,
My manager just told me I am laid off.
Without giving any reason for this ban!
It was so strange of him to ban me in a scoff

MR. TCHINDA

Oh, fairest queen, brightest of the night.
The life we live on earth is like a flight.
Others may choose to fly first class, Others economy, but we are still on the same flight.
A bird at hand is worth a thousand in the bush. Cheer up—Bereaved, not your faith—
Allow not your happiness to be ambushed!

MISS ANGEL

The payload has finally been dropped!

MR. TCHINDA

It has been dropped, but it will flop!

MISS ANGEL

Now, villainy is obvious.
Only cowards are villainous!

MR. TCHINDA

Villains are cowards,
Cowards are envious,
Coward villains are obvious!

MISS ANGEL

What a world, where evil reigns,
Terror rules and rains!

MR. TCHINDA

There's still hope for any tree,
Though cut, but whose roots are in the soil.
We will stand our grounds till evil will flee,
Though it might look rotten or spoiled.

MISS ANGEL

The Lord is our shepherd…

MR. TCHINDA

We shall not want!

MISS ANGEL

He makes us lie down,

MR. TCHINDA

In green pastures!

MISS ANGEL

He leads us…

MR. TCHINDA

Besides the still waters,
He refreshes our souls!

MISS ANGEL

Though we walk through the valley…

MR. TCHINDA

We shall fear no evil!

MISS ANGEL

Have you eaten!

MR. TCHINDA

No, I haven't eaten,
Just beaten, bitten and smitten!

MISS ANGEL

Let it rain tonight and forever!

MR. TCHINDA

(in chorus)

Let it rain cats and dogs!

MISS ANGEL

Let it rain tonight as never.

MR. TCHINDA

(in chorus)

Let it rain cats and dogs!

MISS ANGEL

I will crawl and coil on your arm,
Like a knight would hold his firearm.

MR. TCHINDA

(in chorus)

Let it rain cats and dogs!

MISS ANGEL

A million time, I will kiss your lips
And let your hands caress my hips

MR. TCHINDA

(in chorus)

Let it rain cats and dogs!

MISS ANGEL

A will tell you the story of Adam and Eve,
And the holy fruit in riddles and parables!

MR. TCHINDA

(in chorus)

Let it rain cats and dogs!

MISS ANGEL

If you chose to be an explorer,
And decides to explore all the mountains!

MR. TCHINDA

(in chorus)

Let it rain cats and dogs!

MISS ANGEL

If you're hungry or thirsty
But feel not as to eat or drink any wine,
But choose to drink from my feeding bottles.

MR. TCHINDA

(in chorus)

Let it rain cats and dogs!

MISS ANGEL

The Lord is our shepherd.

MR. TCHINDA

We shall not want!

MISS ANGEL

He makes us lie down,

MR. TCHINDA

In green pastures!

MISS ANGEL

He leads us.

MR. TCHINDA

Besides the still waters,
He refreshes our souls!

(lights gradually fades)

EXIT

ACT 4—SCENE 4

INT. MISS ASUNDER'S MANSION - DAY

Miss Beatrice enters.

MISS ASUNDER

Did the trap catch the mouse,
Or the mouse was finally roused
And had to runway from the house?

MISS BEATRICE

Neither did the trap catch the mouse,
Nor the mouse caught the trap.
Both were all snared and all entrapped.
In a heated and hitted argument, so unpleasant!
As you insinuated, he finally left my house,
And I wandering and wondering as a peasant!

MISS ASUNDER

The plan with Angel's manager was successful,
She's laid off; now I am certain remorseful.

MISS BEATRICE

Hope she learns, next time to be careful,
Not to venture into the unknown forcefully,

Else—she spends her days in hell regretful.
How did you go about so wisely or artfully?

MISS ASUNDER

Some men are like dogs,
Give them bones for them to leap as frogs.
It wasn't an easy task at first or tussle.
Some think with brains, others with muscles,
While others think with their middle leg.
Angel's manager is a dog type or a sparrow,
Brainless, muscle-less, but a type of middle leg.
In his Canterbury Tales, Chaucer says it well,
"Lecherous as a sparrow," he spoke of him,
Back in the days, he wanted to be my boyfriend,
He did not look like a man I could befriend,
Not only so, he was an outcast, not of my caste.
We finally became good friend, never intimate
Though he had always wanted us to relate

MISS BEATRICE

How did you get him to accept the deal,
Tell me the sweet story, haste to unseal!

MISS ASUNDER

I promised him to feed his middle leg,
From starvation, also he loves eating egg.
I also promise him cash—part of my nest egg.
His middle leg is too short, tiny as spaghetti
So tiny as to pass through the eye of a needle.
Now I know why his seven wives divorced him,
Though he claims a man, no fulfilled guarantee.

(Laughing haughtily and mockingly at Martin)

MISS ASUNDER

(Continues)

He's a one-second super-man,
Throat yogurt makes him oink, squeal,
Grunt and growl like a pig on maternity labor.
Guess what?

MISS BEATRICE

Ride-on!

MISS ASUNDER

Then he sleeps off,
Snoring like a train engine,
Or steam locomotive after miles' journey.

MISS BEATRICE

How are you coping with his spaghetti,
When seven-woman had to quit the game
With the shame—

MISS ASUNDER

As you rightly said, it's all a game!
We play it; differently others groan,
Others simply mourn and moan,
While others like myself fake it loud.
It turns him on; he feels like flying in the cloud.

(Laughing haughtily and mockingly at Martin)

MISS ASUNDER

At this point, he thinks,
He's double-clicking the mouse!
Or I am riding the wave!

MISS BEATRICE

I feel for him—foolish moron!
He needs some pills for enlargement
That might help his spaghetti become a python.
How long is this lease or engagement?
Let him not take it as an everlasting marathon!

MISS ASUNDER

I gave him a month lease at least,
It began the moment he fired angel,
Well—I can't wait for the lease to cease.

MISS ASUNDER

I hope he won't ask for an extended lease!

MISS ASUNDER

I promised him a bonus—
A farewell kiss of peace!
Can he afford a woman like me, please!

MISS BEATRICE

Girl, you're a player!
Not just a good player, a plier
That can pinch and bend any hard layer.

MISS ASUNDER

Tchinda is one in a kind,
Sometimes I doubt if his middle leg is fine,
Some men look at me and get so blind,
Blind in lust and loss of peace of mind!
Tchinda is a man difficult to confined,
Or have his mind and love quarantined.

MISS BEATRICE

His middle leg must be active,
This might be the reason why he's attractive,
To Miss Angel—who finds it fantastic.

MISS ASUNDER

He must love a unique taste—romantic
I still ponder how, which style, dramatic
Would he consider to be so seductive,
To resist a woman of my type so acrobatic.

MISS BEATRICE

Like other men, he too is vulnerable,
If not, angel won't be so comfortable,
If she can't spend time with him so memorable.

MISS ASUNDER

Maybe, for now, it is love endurable,
Still hoping to get to that love pleasurable.
Where they will spend eternity inolvidable.

MISS BEATRICE

Tchinda is like a pet tied to a rope,
He can't go beyond this rope,
Even if he runs as fast as an antelope.
He's within reach of my telescope,
I am his remedy, of course, a proctoscope.
All his attempts are forlorn hope!

MISS BEATRICE

You're right,
I am not sure he and angel will cope,
More so, with such an economic upheaval,
They will all gyrate round like a gyroscope,
Until they finally give up hope.

MISS ASUNDER

The bittocks can't be so proud,
To say it does not need a chair.

MISS BEATRICE

A man who uses his manhood to pee,
Shouldn't be proud; it has a second function.
If he doesn't know the second function,
Then he's a fool at the junction.

MISS ASUNDER

I am the chair!

MISS BEATRICE

(in chorus)

He's the buttocks.

MISS ASUNDER

He owns the first function of his manhood

MISS BEATRICE

(in chorus)

But you own the second function.

MISS ASUNDER

I am the air—

MISS BEATRICE

(in chorus)

That he breathes!

MISS ASUNDER

I am the woman—

MISS BEATRICE

He needs!

MISS ASUNDER

If a trap cannot catch a mouse

MISS BEATRICE

The mouse will catch the trap!

MISS ASUNDER

Let's wait and see

EXIT

ACT 4—SCENE 5

INT. PASTOR TYLER'S OFFICE - EVENING

Miss Angel and Mr. Tchinda enter Pastor Tyler's office after church service on Sunday morning.

MISS ANGEL

I've been through the ordeal of Job,
Since I got laid off my job!

PASTOR TYLER

Have you been praying lately?

MISS ANGEL

Yes, I have been praying lately.

PASTOR TYLER

Well—you need to cheer up-
We can't give up!

MISS ANGEL

The world is such a vicious circle,
With evil men having vicious a cycle.

PASTOR TYLER

Flesh and blood, we don't wrestle,
So must we train our spirit not to nestle,
But be able to see evil, crush them or pestle,
Them with God's word or epistles.

MISS ANGEL

When will evil stop to exist?
When they seem to increase and persist?

PASTOR TYLER

There's a day for their doom,
Make sure you don't them room.
We just have one issue at stake,
Our treasurer traveled out of state,
Perhaps, would you mind the position?

MISS ANGEL

Well—A desperate drowning cat,
Never mind reaching out to a rat
If that suffices survival and calms his wrath.

PASTOR TYLER

Your needs will be provided from above.

MISS ANGEL

Amen!

PASTOR TYLER

(Asking Miss Angel about Tchinda)

Who's this gentleman?

MISS ANGEL

He's my fiancé.

PASTOR TYLER

(Surprised)

Are you already affianced!

MISS ANGEL

Yes, I am!

MISS ANGEL

A poet and playwright,
You will read his books with delight!

PASTOR TYLER

(Surprised)

Really!
I will love to have a copy!

Miss Angel gets a copy from her bag, then hands it to Pastor Tyler.

PASTOR TYLER

Thanks!
Nice meeting you, sir!

MR. TCHINDA

My pleasure!

Pastor Tyler takes the book, turns to the back of it, and reads Tchinda's biography and the book synopsis. He lifts his head and looks at Tchinda, and nods in speechless approval from time to time. Then he smiles, puts the book gently on the take.

PASTOR TYLER

The book has some emotional conflicts,
Good for movie adaptation on Neflix!

MISS ANGEL

You're right!

MR. TCHINDA

A tale of civil rights struggles,
In a contentious sue-happy society,
Where people do things by fear or anxiety.
The evil behind the law resides, justice guggles
In favor of the whites, who embark with pride
To oppress the depressed and depress the oppressed.

Pastor Tyler nods his head and clears his throat.

PASTOR TYLER

What's your view or perception,
Of the eight clergymen whose preconception,
Of Martin Luther was seen as "unwise."
"outside agitator," which Luther saw otherwise,
In his "The Negro Is Your Brother"
(April 16, 1963)?

MR. TCHINDA

These eight clergymen
Of course, not eight wisemen.
The court was their priority for liberalism,
Which to Luther was not idealism,
Since the courthouse in his favoritism,
Of white supremacy, racism, or classicism
Will not act right to everyone's right

MISS ANGEL

The eight clergies were all erroneous
A quest for equality was euphonious,
To the court who saw it as felonious.
Whites have always been sanctimonious,
The black protest was more acrimonious,
Even today, is policing not unceremonious?

PASTOR TYLER

In today's American society,
With so much panic and anxiety,
What will Martin Luther address,
Or what needs to be redressed?

MR. TCHINDA

He will see to address our democrazy,
To be redressed back to democracy!

Pastor Tyler laughs mercilessly.

MISS ANGEL

You can't trust the police anymore,
When they stop you on the road,
If you happen to smile mistakenly.

MR. TCHINDA

They will assume.
They will shoot you with haste hate.

MISS ANGEL

You can't trust the police anymore,
When they stop you on the road,
When they grope your double cherry pie,
And you get vexed or frown, or moan.

MR. TCHINDA

They will assume.
They will shoot you with haste hate.

MISS ANGEL

You can't trust the police anymore,
When they stop you on the road,
When she gropes the little man in the boat,
And you get vexed or frown, or moan.

MR. TCHINDA

They will assume.
They will shoot you with haste hate.

MISS ANGEL

You can't trust the police anymore,
When they stop you on the road,
If you nod your head in disapproval.

MR. TCHINDA

They will assume.
They will shoot you with haste hate.

MISS ANGEL

You can't trust the police anymore,
When they stop you on the road,
If you they say "we're sick,"
And if you say no, "you're sick."

MR. TCHINDA

They will assume.
They will shoot you with haste and hate

MISS ANGEL

You can't trust the police anymore,
If the police know that you breathe,
And they know that you're black,

MR. TCHINDA

They will assume.
They will shoot you with haste hate

MISS ANGEL

Did we not fight for freedom together,
Or must all we all be killed all together?
Aren't we supposed to love one another?

MR. TCHINDA

A man who read his epistles,
And also wrote an epistolary,
"Letter from Birmingham City Jail,"
"The Negro is your brother."
Only demanded our 340 rights.

MISS ANGEL

They assumed,
They shot him in haste, hate, and waste!

PASTOR TYLER

So proud of you all.
Let's pray...

EXIT

ACT 5—SCENE 1

NARRATOR

(Off Stage)

A perfect gentleman and follower of Christ,
So devout to his self-piety to be evil enticed,
Such a man to have in your or every congregation,
Permit me to introduce him to you all, James.
I am sure he was named after Saint James.
It's not proper to suggest or call people names,
You will soon discover during these Olympic games
The truth of religious goers or messianic confession claims.
Sometimes I think we've lost our minds or brains.
Light begets light; evil begets evil, simple truth alike.
Whatever a man sows, so does he reap be like,
Everyone claims of a divine soul and knows Christ's dislike
We now profess holiness and heavenward dreamlike,
And think we're better than others in hunger strike,
Because we have abundance, just as every pharisee.
There is one fate that awaits us all, be it Christian or Sadducee
At the end of our pilgrimage here on earth,
Where we shall stand the great Armageddon of rebirth,
And give an account of our lives to Elohim.
It will be at your discretion to judge of him,
A gentleman who ends up preyed in Asunder's scheme

And let his righteous and spiritual light grow dim
He is more of a church verb, proverb, or a synonym
Who can do anything, accept anything such as a pseudonym
To meet his needs in misdeeds. What a disgrace to the hymn,
Which he sings every day as an angel of light!
Such individuals have robbed the salt of the earth of its delight
Don't get distracted and miss your flight,
Everyone has an individual heavenward flight,
Life is a battle; we must aim to righteously fight,
Access not every access even at a green light.
Greenlight to some access requires insight
Insight to access a green light requires foresight
Foresight to assess or access any green light despite
All the pleasures it might bring or lure us into.
I have much to say; there is "Much Ado About Nothing,"
I am confused and fused, without further ado, adieu!

EXT. STREET IN HARLEM, NEW YORK CITY - DAY

Later that same Sunday evening, Mr. James, the former restaurant attendant, meets Miss Asunder on her way to Miss Beatrice's apartment at Lenox Avenue, Harlem, New York City. Miss Asunder had parked her car to get some stuff from the store. On her entry into her vehicle, she then sees Mr. James walking with his head down as a pauper thinking about his next meal to eat. He is holding his Bible in his left hand.

MISS ASUNDER

James!

Miss Asunder yells his name and waives at him. Mr. James, upon hearing his name, turns and recognizes the voice. His face is lightened as he walks gradually to meet her by her car.

MR. JAMES

Sorry,
I was dead and buried in thought,
I didn't hear you, only an after-thought?

MISS ASUNDER

Don't let your thoughts,
Become a vicious blind spot.
Are you jogging to dome sport?

MR. JAMES

You're right; my mind is wrought!

MISS ASUNDER

Rough?
Well—don't go nut,
The sun overhead is too hot!

MR. JAMES

Things have been so lumpy,
Since I lost my job, life is so grumpy!

MISS ASUNDER

What did transpire,
That the restaurant caught fire,
And drew city attention as a campfire?

MR. JAMES

We still don't know what backfired,
It's assumed a gas cooker by a livewire,
Might have sparked the wildfire,

Which consumed everything to a flat tire.

MISS ASUNDER

I am sure you had insurance!

She rushes into her car, opens the front seat compartment, and brings it out. Looking at the newspaper again, she nods in disapproval.

MR. JAMES

Yes, but of now, no assurance.

MISS ASUNDER

Why?

MR. JAMES

They claimed the fire was intentional.

MISS ASUNDER

That's why I hate insurance,
They give you false hope of assurance,
They will give you long terms of assurance,
Feed you with lies of long-term assurance,
Until a D-day when you see deterrence.

MR. JAMES

They're all thieves and crooks,
Two days after the fire incident
My car got into a fatal car accident,
I survived, but my car didn't survive.
I call them that my car wasn't in good looks,
They wrote it down in their notebooks,
But refused to pay for the damages.

MISS ASUNDER

Did you get a lawyer,
One who is genuine and loyal?

MR. JAMES

Better buying plane than hiring a lawyer.

Miss Asunder smiles. *She reaches into her handbag, gives him three hundred dollars, two bills of a hundred dollars and two bills of fifty dollars, brand new as if they have never been used before?*

MR. JAMES

I am grateful,
This day has been faithful and fateful.

MISS ASUNDER

I wish we could make it eventful?
I have to see my friend, something useful
Call me anytime, if I can be helpful

(About to depart)

MR. JAMES

Do you remember the gentleman?

MISS ASUNDER

Which one?

MR. JAMES

At the restaurant, who bills you paid?

MISS ASUNDER

Yes, I know—yes, I do!
What happened?

MISS ASUNDER

I saw them in the church today,
When going, we meet on our way.

Asunder begins to blush, heart panting.

JAMES

(continues)

He was with the other lady.

MISS ASUNDER

How was she, shady?

MR. JAMES

Neither shady, shabby, but chubby!

MISS ASUNDER

It's becoming hot; we get to the car?
I feel on heat; I am feeling the heat,
I feel the heat hit, and the hit heat hit!
Very soon, a scar!

MR. JAMES

Sorry, madame, I am in a haste,
I am trying to keep with time pace,
If I can get another job by his grace!

MISS ASUNDER

Please, don't haste,
I will redeem your time,
Time is money, but I am worth than money,
Tell me more, where are they traced?
I'll build the ruins of your life now in waste.
If you let me know where they're based.

MR. JAMES

Yes, ma'am,
I will be more than pleased!

MISS ASUNDER

Please, put aside my fame,
Call me by my name!

MR. JAMES

Ok, ma'am!
Sorry—Asunder!

MISS ASUNDER

Where are they traced?

MR. JAMES

I am uncertain of their base,
But in church, they are retraced!

MISS ASUNDER

Can you undress me the address?

MR. JAMES

With much largesse!
Here's the full address,
You'll find them, faith obsessed!

MISS ASUNDER

What of the days of attendance?

MR. JAMES

(Pulling a flyer with the church information, hands it to Asunder)

I hope this speaks volumes!

MISS ASUNDER

You're such a sweetheart,
Don't you have any sweat heart?

MR. JAMES

I have one-Miss Envy
Our love for one another is weighty,
Hopefully, we mingle soon,
Now with income lost, uncertainty is soon!

MISS ASUNDER

I have your back,
This is just the Genesis of my generosity,
When we get to the revelation of my luminosity
You will understand its ponderosity.

MISS ASUNDER

Wow!
I feel in a paradise city!

MISS ASUNDER

Not paradise city, but parasite city!
A city of parasite and paradise!

MR. JAMES

At your disposal—anytime!

MISS ASUNDER

And also—anywhere

Miss Asunder reaches out to her handbag and gives him another three hundred dollars. This time, the bills are sparkling than the previous ones.

EXIT

ACT 5—SCENE 2

NARRATOR

(Off Stage)

Deep in my heart, too, I have a grudge
Against my old boyfriend, pastor Judge.
He used to preach on holiness and fire,
But he was like a dog on fire,
Who won't see any "budussy" come by!
Since his bible and "little guy" stood by.
He will change his sermon for a "poontang pie."
Even for a Gucci bible, or "coochie bible."
He was indeed possessed for a pussycat,
And loved to see pussycats with a black hat.
He was of libido, "sexcess," so excessive,
A type very rare, obsessive—aggressive,
One morning, he found his demise,
In a harlot's house, in and by her "badussy."
Who knows, perhaps he died a "pussi" stroke.
He was very handsome, of age sixty-nine,
He was hot, "sassy," obsessed with "sixty-nine"!
He was a virtuous pastor, a generous giver,
He had good taste; he loved eating "beaver,"
Then, he will praise God every "mornincation."
He had a pet name; I called him "morningasm,"

Since he'll preach against sin with sarcasm.
He was always eating "breakfast -of-champions,"
He was a scholar of the "morning constitution,"
He craved for "morning treatment" than the Bible,
He was all in one, a gifted chef always able,
To please his church, even "cooking pancakes,"
To please them, since they also loved "seggs."
I loved God, but he "made my love come down"!
He had an "o-spot" car, parked downtown.
He preached like thunder, sometimes scream,
When he felt too much anointing, he'll "cream,"
But it will not stop from "going all the way."
He had a good "mussy" and loved prophecy,
The spirit of his prophecy will "power u."
To praise him, like a choirmaster in "egasm."
He went from house to house, all his way,
To cast devils and demons of "mouthgasm."
Once delivered, he will praise God "afterglow."
He even won the best demon chaser "Oscar."
As he was named "twilight" superstar.
He was sometimes mistakenly for a dentist,
His teeth were all aligned like a "camel's toe."
But he claims he was also a gospel artist.
His best praise song was "jizzy woo woo,"
Where he spent all tithes and offerings.
That's when you see his teeth, brown and old.

May his soul rest in perfect peace!

INT. MISS BEATRICE'S APARTMENT - EVENING

Miss Asunder enters, looking unhappy.

MISS ASUNDER

They've now joined a religion,
They're always there as a paired pigeon.
Somewhere, not far from Lenox Avenue,
Where their church is located, worship venue.

MISS BEATRICE

Is religion not like opium?
They've chosen to err rightly with a podium,
A placed for the brainwashed and odium,
Who struggle to quit with their past guilt,
Just a matter of time from now,
They will be like rats and will bow!

MISS ASUNDER

They seem to be doing so well,
Angel looks chubby and very belle!

MISS BEATRICE

It's all camouflage; we know it all,
All that glitters is not gold; it will fall.
Just a matter of time to see their jaws shrink,
Their doom is near, just an eyeblink.

MISS ASUNDER

Their glamor or glitter is beyond gold.
As I was being informed and told,

By someone who knows them, of old,
Who told me this truth, nothing to withhold.

MISS BEATRICE

Telling you is not seeing.
Faith is the ability to foresee
Things before they happen or occur.
I don't believe in hearsay; I abhor
Such tales until I see it occur or incur.

MISS ASUNDER

Our former bar attendant, James.
He now worships there, a kind of St. James.
We can get him onboard our scheme,
He's a sweetheart, a man of low esteem,
Who will accept anything, even an ice scream
For any task that will help his dream.

MISS BEATRICE

Is he reliable, pliable, and able?
Not somebody of noble like Abel,
But someone who can act like Cain,
Who fears no flogging even with a cane.

MISS ASUNDER

At this moment and hour, we speak,
He's jobless and is also in Job's ordeal,
He's at my disposal with a submissive zeal,
A zeal to do anything, anything so bleak.

MISS BEATRICE

Money speaks—money is the key,
That opens doors of all sizes, small or big.
Let's try him; he looks like a good guinea pig,
Let's use him as a spade to plow and dig!

MISS ASUNDER

Of course, he is a parishioner there
We need an informant to lead us into a dare,
Without having someone to lead us or guide
Our plans might die, capsize or even subside!

MISS BEATRICE

A hungry man is an angry man,
A hungry man isn't superman,
A hungry superman can become a bad man!

MISS ASUNDER

Why not also become members,
Since churches are always desperate
To have new people add to numbers,
Big tithes and offerings make them elate.

MISS BEATRICE

Aren't we going to suspicious?

MISS ASUNDER

Do we have masks to look suspicious?

MISS BEATRICE

Well—nothing pernicious,
Churches themselves are auspicious,
Whet the pastor's lip with tithes, delicious,
He will sell the sheep cheap to ferocious
Bargainers, even if they look inauspicious!

MISS ASUNDER

Some pastors are themselves like sheep,
When they see money, they bleat so deep!
Some pastors are themselves like dogs,
Some are real dogs; they bark like dogs,
When a new bitch comes in like a sheep!

MISS BEATRICE

We're holy; let's not bother to judge

MISS ASUNDER

Let them carry their cross,
Tchinda is my only concern, and cross
I wish he were a pussy-man I came across
For me to crucify him on my cross.

Miss Asunder stumbles on one of Tchinda's picture on Miss Beatrice's wall. She walks closer to look at the picture. It's the picture of when they picked him up from the airport.

MISS BEATRICE

Are you taking a deeper gaze!

MISS ASUNDER

He's just a sweet as a glaze!
He's my gaze and glaze!

MISS ASUNDER

Out of sight, never out of mind!

MISS BEATRICE

Do you need one for enlargement?
Faith is an unforeseen engagement.

MISS ASUNDER

You're right.
I will enchant his name and spirit.
I will be able to connect to his aura's light

MISS BEATRICE

Draw the devil on the wall
And he will appear at your demand.

MISS ASUNDER

I don't need the devil to appear,
In Angel's heart, I want him to disappear.

EXIT

ACT 5—SCENE 3

INT. PASTOR TYLER'S OFFICE - EVENING

Pastor Tyler is looking through the church balance sheet. He nods his head in approval as he opens the financial record page by page. Everything is correct. He suddenly shuts the book, puts it in his drawer, fixes his eyes on Miss Angel.

PASTOR TYLER.

Keep up, I am impressed!

MISS ANGEL

Thanks!

PASTOR TYLER

(clearing his throat)

Is your fiancé born again?

MISS ANGEL

Yes, but not for gain!

PASTOR TYLER

He doesn't look like,
Nor one who plays games!

MISS ANGEL

I watched and prayed,
I prayed and watched,
Now, I watch not to be preyed.

PASTOR TYLER

There is the evil behind the law,
The sting of death is sin,
The power of sin and crime is the law

MISS ANGEL

Though evil lurks behind the law,
We still need the law.

PASTOR TYLER

You're right,
What of back codes laws?

Tchinda enters, pulls a seat by Miss Angel, and joins the Conversation

MISS ANGEL

Black codes are still in our hearts
That's why our hearts are hard!

MR. TCHINDA

Do we think to have gone a long way?
We're still halfway—
Let's look at where we came from;
1863—Emancipation proclamation
1865—Reconstruction Era begins
1866—Ku Klux Klan is born

1870-1871—Enforcement Acts
1875—Civil Rights Acts
1877—End of Reconstruction Era
1883—Civil Rights Acts Declared unconstitutional
1896—Plessy V. Ferguson
1898—The Wilmington Race Riot
1906—Atlanta Race Riot
1909—NAAP was born.
1954—Brown V. Board of Education of Topeka.
1965—End of Jim Crow Era.

TCHINDA

(Continues)

Our hearts are bleeding,
Because our history is bleeding.
Our democracy is falling apart,
Because our history is bleeding
Our economy is in chaos
Because innocent blood are weeping,
Oh, great nation of America in decline
Why and how are thou falling?

MISS ANGEL

We've walked a long journey together,
We've fought a common enemy together,
We've written history altogether,
We laid the cornerstone together,
Now...
We deny seeing one another as a brother,
Now...
We deny seeing one another as a sister.

Whereas we began this journey together;
1955—Rosa Parks vs. Montgomery Bus Boycott
1957—The Little Rock Nine.
1960—The Greensboro Four.
1960—Ruby Bridges.
1961—Freedom Rides.
1963—Birmingham Demonstrations
1963—March on Washington
1964—Civil Right Act
1965—Assassination of Malcolm X
1965—Selma-Montgomery March
1965—Watts Riots
1966—Black Panther Party formed
1967—Loving V. Virginia
1967—Detroit Riot
1968—Assassination of Martin Luther King.

MR. TCHINDA

Should we still be fighting the same fight?
When we know; "Black Lives Matter."
Should we still be fighting the same fight?
When we know; "All Men Are Equal."
Should we still be fighting the same fight?
When we know; "All Lives Matter."
I haven't seen a white dog fight a black dog,
I haven't seen a white ant fight a black ant,
I haven't seen a white goat fight a black goat,
But i have seen a white man fights a black man
But i have seen a black man fight a white man.
I have seen both white and black die like animals.
Are we not more than animals?

MISS ANGEL

Our history should teach us.

MR. TCHINDA

Not unteach us—

MISS ANGEL

Our history should teach us to repent.

MR. TCHINDA

Not brag of our racial sins—

MISS ANGEL

Our history should teach us
To love one another.

MR. TCHINDA

Not to hate one another—

MISS ANGEL

Our history should teach us
Our sins and crimes, both blacks and whites

MR. TCHINDA

Not to make all whites saints—
Not to make all blacks criminals—

MISS ANGEL

Our history should teach us
That with the advent of Covid-19.

MR. TCHINDA

Our lives are to the gods,
As sailor's ships are to the Bermuda Triangle—

MISS ANGEL

Our history should teach us
That life is vanity upon vanity.

MR. TCHINDA

Because we shall all die as rats—
Blacks, or whites alike—
No matter how beautiful your grave is,
The earth will be our roof.
No matter if you're a free or slave
The earth will be our roof.
No matter how rich or poor you're
The earth will be our roof.

MISS ANGEL

We shall still see the people we hated,
We shall still see women we raped,
We shall still see the people we killed
We shall still the children killed in rituals

MR. TCHINDA

There are still alive! There are still alive!

MISS ANGEL

We killed their flesh, never their souls!
We imprisoned their bodies.
But never their souls

We deprived them of happiness,
But not joy everlasting!

MR. TCHINDA

We shall live together a free life
Both Tchinda and Angel in Chorus

With no congressional classicism!
With no black codes!
With no dread from and of 911!
With no police rage and brutality!
With no by-word "shite-hole citizens"!

MR. TCHINDA

I will see Martin Luther King;
We will all say; "We Have A Dream."
We will all sing "Black Lives Matter."

MISS ANGEL

I will see Rosa Parks!
We will all say; "We Have A Dream."
We will all sing, "Black Lives Matter."

TCHINDA, ANGEL, AND PASTOR TYLER

(In one chorus)

We shall see—Rayshared Brooks—27 years.
We shall see—Daniel Prude—41 years
We shall see—George Floyd—46 years,
We shall see—Breonna Taylor—26 years,
We shall see—Atatiana Jefferson—28 years
We shall see—Aura Rosser—40 years
We shall see—Stephon Clark—22 years

We shall see—Botham Jean—26 years
We shall see—Philando Castille—32 years
We shall see—Alton Sterling—37 years
We shall see—Michelle Cusseaux—50 years,
We shall see—Freddie Gray—25 years,
We shall see—Janisha Fonville—20 years,
We shall see—2014 Eric Garner—43 years,
We shall see—Akai Gurley—28 years,
We shall see 2014-Gabriella Nevarez—22 years,
We shall see—Tamir Rice—12 years,
We shall see—Michael Brown—18 years?
We shall see—Tanisha Anderson—37 years.

PASTOR TYLER

"Blessed are the poor in spirit."

TCHINDA AND ANGEL

"For theirs is the kingdom of heaven."

PASTOR TYLER

"Blessed are those who mourn."

TCHINDA AND ANGEL

They will be comforted."

PASTOR TYLER

"Blessed are the meek."

TCHINDA AND ANGEL

They shall inherit the earth."

PASTOR TYLER

Blessed…

(Open Vision - Trance)

Listen—
Here is what I see deep in my spirit.
A great war is waged against your union.
I see you crossing a bridge—
A very narrow and long one.
The wind is so strong, tossing the bridge
Left and right. At the end of the bridge
Are figures like angels flapping their wings.
All dressed in white robes.
Then come to a trumpet—a bright rainbow
Yelling. Victory! Victory, Victory!

(end of vision)

PASTOR TYLER

We must pray fervently,
Let's pray…

ACT 5—SCENE 4

INT. MISS ANGEL'S APARTMENT - EVENING

Through the help of Mr. James, Miss Asunder and Miss Beatrice have got the address where Miss Angel and Tchinda now live. It's a newly innovated two-bedroom apartment with modern appliances. The weather is hot as hell outside, but Tchinda's apartment is cold and refreshing enough to retain every guest. Miss Beatrice and Miss Asunder have come pretentiously to ask for an apology.

MISS ANGEL

I see war coming to our nest,
We must be ready for what's next?
It's like fire, glowing as a campfire!
Something is about to transpire.

MR. TCHINDA

It's fire; indeed, it only glows,
The more it glows, the more our love grows,
Fire is good for the heart; it doesn't burn,
It purifies, true love sometimes is earned.

MISS ANGEL

Bae, your right in your saying,
But this is what is am saying,
I see and scent fire, fire not too far!

MR. TCHINDA

I am hotter than fire,
I have been refined by fire
I have been defined by fire
What can fire do to fire?

The doorbell rings.

MISS ANGEL

Are you waiting for any guest!

Mr. Tchinda heads to the door. Miss Angel exits to the room. The door opens, and Miss Beatrice and Miss Asunder then enter.

MR. TCHINDA

No guest, I guess!

MISS ASUNDER

Are we welcomed?

MR. TCHINDA

You're welcome, but not home!
What vice are you planning next?

MISS BEATRICE

Please, tame your temperament!
I know your heart Is sore in resentment
Now, I am broken in heart and born anew,
Please, let's go the past in its rear view
And turn a new page of love and forgiveness
So that I can gain back my aliveness.

MR. TCHINDA

I am proud to hear such from your lips,
A tongue so gentle with words so drip,
Hate is not my temperament; love is.
I hope you did come in peace?

MISS BEATRICE

We came to seek peace,
If you grant us your peace,
We will be at ease and feel at peace,

MR. TCHINDA

What is don't?

MISS BEATRICE

We remain broken in pieces!

MISS ASUNDER

Hi—Tchinda!

MR. TCHINDA

Hi, Asunder!

MISS BEATRICE

Can we come in, please?

MR. TCHINDA

Yes, come-on in?

Miss Asunder's eyes race the wall, and she sees Tchinda's picture with Miss Angel hanging. She then quickly struggles to gulp her jealousy.

MISS BEATRICE

Your girlfriend looks pretty!

MR. TCHINDA

Thanks!

MISS ASUNDER

Like an angel from the Vatican City!

MISS ANGEL

(re-enters)

What a surprising visit!
I hope it's for good elicit.

MISS ASUNDER

Very elicit and licit!

MISS ANGEL

If it's elicit and licit,
What do I gain from this visit!

MISS ASUNDER

We're sinners seeking for your clemency,
We know we're not worthy of being here,
As the good book says, be at peace
With all men. Our wrongs are heavy to bear,
As a good shepherdess, please hear
Our broken hearts, and contrite spirits.
With humility, here I go on my knees,
To remorse for my past, and misdeeds.

MISS BEATRICE

Dearest and fairest of all virtue,
I'm also to my knees; we've hurt you,
We know your heart bleeds and beats
But we've come to remorse for our misdeeds.

MISS ASUNDER

My heart is pure, free from hate,
Search your hearts, from your pate,
Down the sole of your feet,
If you stand clean, as you thus confess,
I've never hated you, what do I benefit?

MISS BEATRICE

You're a true embodiment of light,
Beyond my imagination and sight,
You're blessed to be my brother's wife,
Whom I have offended in bitter strife.

MR. TCHINDA

Life is all vanity upon vanity,
The things we fight for or seek for today,
We shall all die, leave behind someday.
For those who did not fight for,
For those who did not kill for,
For those who did not murder for.
For those who didn't seek for
To enjoy and live happy.

MISS ANGEL

Samuel Taylor Coleridge
Lived on, but has moved on.

MR. TCHINDA

October 21, 1772–July 25, 1834.

MISS ANGEL

Percy Bysshe Shelley
Lived on, but has moved on.

MR. TCHINDA

August 4, 1792–July 8, 1822

MISS ANGEL

Robert Burns
Lived on, but has moved on.

MR. TCHINDA

January 25, 1759–July 21, 1796

MISS ANGEL

John Keats
Lived on, but has moved on.

MR. TCHINDA

October 31, 1795–February 23, 1821

MISS ANGEL

Victor Hugo
Lived on, but has moved on.

MR. TCHINDA

October 31, 1795–February 23, 1821

MISS ANGEL

William Wordsworth
Lived on, but has moved on.

MR. TCHINDA

April 7, 1770–April 23, 1850

MISS ANGEL

William Wordsworth,
Lived on, but has moved on.

MR. TCHINDA

November 28, 1757–August 12, 1827

MISS ANGEL

Is life not all vanity?

TCHINDA, BEATRICE, AND ASUNDER

(In chorus)

It's vanity upon vanity.

MR. TCHINDA

Beatrice, we have forgiven you!

MISS ANGEL

We've paid you all that we owed, love!

EXIT

ACT 5—SCENE 5

INT. CHURCH AT HARLEM, NEW YORK - DAY

The choir is singing. Prophecy then begins. Miss Beatrice, Miss Asunder, and Miss Angel enter.

PASTOR TYLER

The devil has dared the battle line
Parishioners are murmuring

PASTOR TYLER

Be watchful, pray, and resist him.

MISS BEATRICE

Do you see the devil?

MISS ASUNDER

No,
I don't see anybody.
Perhaps he is hallucinating.

PASTOR TYLER

What God has put together,
Let no one put asunder.

MISS ASUNDER

He seems to talk to me.

MISS BEATRICE

Are you a devil?

MISS ASUNDER

No!

MISS BEATRICE

Then why do you fear?
He said resist him, not her!
So you cannot be the devil
He's preaching about.

PASTOR TYLER

Repent, or your plans will fail.
I am the Alpha and Omega.

End of prophecy. The parishioner's exit. Outside the church, there are discussions in groups.

MISS ANGEL

I'm persuaded with reason,
And inward conviction this season,
Asunder and Beatrice are still capricious.

MR. TCHINDA

They have always been capricious,
I know they're still pretentious,
Though they claim conscientious.

MISS ANGEL

Caution is needed,
They haven't still conceded!

MR. TCHINDA

They've crossed the battle line,
It doesn't define victory.
In the end, there is a baseline,
That defines victory for our love.

MISS ANGEL

You're right, my king,
The line between light and darkness,
Good and evil always seem alike!

Mr. Tchinda and Miss Angel exit. Mr. James, Miss Beatrice, and Miss Asunder enter the Pastor's office.

MR. JAMES

Pastor, we have an addition,
Saved mysteriously from perdition!

PASTOR TYLER

Praise be to our father,
Our doors are open wide for you
Let's know what you can do.

MISS ASUNDER

You're a man of God on fire,
This season, all my foes will backfire!

MISS BEATRICE

Amen!

MISS ASUNDER

No weapon formed against us…

MISS BEATRICE

Amen!

MISS ASUNDER

The Lord is my shepherd,
I shall not want—

MISS BEATRICE

Amen!

MISS ASUNDER

He prepares a table before me,
In front of my enemies

MISS BEATRICE

Amen!

PASTOR TYLER

I see you're on fire!

MR. JAMES

Fire brand intercessors.

MISS ASUNDER

He makes his servant's flames of fire.

MISS BEATRICE

Amen!

PASTOR TYLER

What's your names?

MISS ASUNDER

Asunder and Beatrice

PASTOR TYLER

Wow!
So unique, asunder!

MISS ASUNDER

I was chosen from my mother's womb,
And set apart by the Lord!

MISS BEATRICE

Amen!

MISS ASUNDER

Pastor, I have my tithes,
My first seed, pray for me.

PASTOR TYLER

May the Lord bless you!

MISS ASUNDER

Amen!

PASTOR TYLER

May he give you an increase!

MISS ASUNDER

Amen!

PASTOR TYLER

May he bless your marriage!

MISS BEATRICE

Amen! We receive it!

MISS ASUNDER

Amen!
I bind any woman from my fiancé.

EXIT

ACT 6—SCENE 1

INT. MISS ASUNDER'S MANSION - DAY

Miss Beatrice and Miss Asunder have successfully got access into the church cycle, where the final wedding preparations are taking place with the church committee's help. They can't win the battle if they are outsiders to the game. Miss Asunder is becoming restless, yet she's still determined to take it to the end.

MISS ASUNDER

We've crossed the battle line,
We can't retreat from victory!
All our plans seem to be aligned,
But the wedding seems not far.
This marriage is just a tale or history.

MISS BEATRICE

Our plans are well aligned,
Now that we're at the threshold,
We must look for an inner stronghold.
We cannot fight just from the outside,
We must fight with someone from the inside.
Someone who has good insight.

MISS ASUNDER

Life itself is a circle, so vicious,
Everyone has their motivations,

Some are true, others superstitious,
What matters to me is the man I love!

MISS BEATRICE

James can be a good devil within,
We can use him to subvert the wedding.

MISS ASUNDER

He's my good puppet,
You just need to toss him a crumpet,
Then you have what you desire.
He's a man already in the mire!

MISS BEATRICE

Have you dropped this to his ears?

MISS ASUNDER

No, but the answer will be yes!
That's simple; it doesn't take me years.

MISS ASUNDER

Why don't you give him a ring,
So that we use him as a string?

MISS ASUNDER

(Dialing his number)

Well—he's not picking his phone!

MISS BEATRICE

He might be out of network!

MISS ASUNDER

Not in such a time when needed,
This plan cannot be impeded,
Or in any way stampeded.

MISS BEATRICE

Tame your temperament,
We will soon be in the merriment!

MISS ASUNDER

Let me drink myself to stupor!
Let's celebrate this victory so superb!

MISS ASUNDER

Let's drink like a fish,
We can't fall for a phish.

MISS BEATRICE

Prophecy has been many's doom,
We can tap from the one this noon.

MISS ASUNDER

How?

MISS ASUNDER

Simple! James will pervert message,
Use it to dissuade Tchinda marriage.

There's an incoming call from Mr. James to Asunder.

MISS ASUNDER

Hello!

MR. JAMES

Hello!
Sorry I missed your call.

MISS ASUNDER

How soon can you haste to place?

MR. JAMES

The next bus schedule is in the next two hours.

MISS ASUNDER

Time is our greatest foe,
Can you do Uber to mt mansion?

MR. JAMES

That's a cost!

MISS ASUNDER

Cost is costless.
Time redemption is a priority.
I have the money; I have the authority,
To buy you a car that cost me less.

MR. JAMES

Please, text me your address!

End of the phone call. Miss Asunder is making a money transfer to Mr. James through CashApp.

MISS ASUNDER

Great! Great minds think alike.

MISS BEATRICE

Many hands make a task lighter,
We might need more than one fighter,
Who will join James to make it tighter.

MISS ASUNDER

Let's get the boss involved.
Once things get revolved,
The rest is history.

Mr. James enters Miss Asunder's mansion.

MISS ASUNDER

Time has spoken well of you,
We have a task only you can do,
Luckily, you're here so on time to do.

MR. JAMES

I am here, at your service!
Any cervix?

MISS ASUNDER

Not too soon,
If that's what you want
You'll get it, even as soon as noon,
For now, let's talk about the hunt!

MR. JAMES

Haunt!

MISS BEATRICE

Yes!
Your finger is still a virgin,
No sugarplum or hootie, I can imagine,
How tight you are pushed to the margin.

MR. JAMES

(Smiling amorously)

Still single to be mingled.

MISS ASUNDER

Don't be shy to be amorlustly or amorustly

MISS BEATRICE

We'll get you a wife if you need one.
It's a need for you, and also a want!

MR. JAMES

At your disposal, any time, any moment!

MISS ASUNDER

What if we made you a good offer,
Would you accept my proffer?

MR. JAMES

What proffer do you offer?

MISS BEATRICE

Any you can think of—
cars, houses, sex, marriage.

MR. JAMES

Prayers are answered in many ways.

MISS ASUNDER

That's why you scratch my back,
Then I will also scratch yours
Straight to the point,
Bathsheba has taken my David in church!

Perplexed upon hearing this, Mr. James gathers himself together and continues.

MR. JAMES

There is no Bathsheba nor David in church.

MISS ASUNDER

Not in our church, but churches!

MISS BEATRICE

Miss Angel and Tchinda.

Mr. James's mouth remains agape, bewildered, and speechless.

MISS ASUNDER

Tchinda is my fiancé
But he's now bewitched by Angel.

MR. JAMES

Miss Asunder,
An eye for an eye, a tooth for a tooth.

MISS ASUNDER

If you conquer my Goliath,
Just as David did, great is your reward,
You can mark or hold me by my word.

MR. JAMES

I am deadly ready.
If you want Miss Angel dead,
I will shred her from toe to head,
Relax, it will be quick and shady!

MISS BEATRICE

Please, don't shed blood,
We're Christians—just asunder!

EXIT

ACT 6—SCENE 2

NARRATOR

(Off Stage)

As once said,
Only daring devil dare to enter where angels dread.
More than little has been said or needs to be unsaid,
A traumatic drama called charismatic witchcraft!
All this in shrines called house of God by men of gods,
Gospel craftsmen, guilty of many sins and bloodshed,
Who claim to preach the gospel but read and mislead
The lost souls of Christ, repent of all your misdeeds.

The gospel is now of no effect, Christians like riffraff,
No doubt thieves now carry the Bible as a craft
Not to save souls but to feed on innocent blood.
From their evil manipulation or gospel stage craft.
I am not a judge, but I have a grudge
I am against us, who preach to others to adjust,
But is lost in pride, immorality, lust in disgust.

Haste to repent when light shines, soon will be dusk,
You might not have time to adjust to the rust and lust
For money, which, is vanishing vanity like dust,
From which we shall return to rest to rust.

Strife for mercy, not all-knowing prophet or seer,
The papa of all, the mega-church papa apostle
Who desires titles and tithes, even ready to jostle.

Christ desires brokenness of heart than sacrifice,
He's paid the sacrifice for our bride price,
He just wants you to follow him, good deeds to be precise.
Stand aright with him; don't think too wise,
Don't yield your bodies for the devil's vices,
Like Beatrice and Asunder in a fool's paradise,

Claiming justice by the law, fairness, and of it brag.
A way seems right to man, but beware of red a flag
Human laws control the body, other laws beyond that,
Love one another, with one love, not as a doormat.
You leave this world to face your fate or combat.
Life beyond is now, now is the time to be ready.

INT. THE CHURCH- EVENING

Miss Asunder and Miss Beatrice are seated in front seats. There are dressed so flamboyantly with excessive make-up and eyelashes like broomsticks.

PASTOR TYLER

The devil and his disciples are at work
Disguised innocently as angels of light,
Calm and deceitful as an angel-shark,
But mortal than a great white shark!
So addicted to evil, they're ready to smite.

The parishioners are murmuring.

PASTOR TYLER

Beware for the love of money.
Though funny, it leads to agony.
Beware and be warned!

PASTOR TYLER

Tchinda and Angel will soon say,
"Yes, I do" for life!

Pastor Tyler asks Miss Angel and Mr. Tchinda to come in front of the church for a general presentation. They move forward, and Pastor Tyler unintentionally asks them to stand just one meter from where Miss Asunder and Miss Beatrice are sitting. Parishioners are yelling in merriment. The church drummer, out of excitement, beats the drums mercilessly. The choir joins in the chorus, and the parishioners answer the chorus from behind.

PASTOR TYLER

The wedding has not begun.
But we see the glory has risen,
And can't be stopped for any reason.

The parishioners are murmurings.

PASTOR TYLER

What God has put together,
Now and forever…

PARISHIONERS

(In chorus)

Let no one put asunder,
Now and forever…

PASTOR TYLER

Pray for them often,
The devil has, and his disciples have Entered the church with hardened hearts.

MISS BEATRICE

Let's bind them!

MISS ASUNDER

Well—even in the days of Job,
Wasn't satan in God's presence doing his job?

PASTOR TYLER

There is time for everything under the sun,
A time to love and a time to hate,
A time to go fast and a time to haste,
A time to be single and a time to mingle,
A time to merry and a time to marry

PARISHIONERS

(In chorus)

Amen!

PASTOR TYLER

Husbands, love your wives.
Wives, submit to your husbands,
Don't become registered nurses,
Then become to your husband's knives.
Husbands, women love big purses…

PARISHIONERS

(In chorus)

Amen!

PASTOR TYLER

Love one another, bear no grudge!
Don't steal, what isn't your, don't budge!
Don't judge others, be just and adjust.

PARISHIONERS

(In chorus)

Amen!

PASTOR TYLER

Don't be quick to judge; you'll misjudge!
Be outspoken, don't be a back judge.
Be holy; sin makes your soul trudge.
Don' envy one's husband or wife.
You might end up losing your own life.

PARISHIONERS

(In chorus)

Amen!

PASTOR TYLER

Whatever you sow, you'll reap.

PARISHIONERS

(In chorus)

Amen!

PASTOR TYLER

Stand to your feet and lift your hands.
Pray for Mr. Tchinda and Miss Angel.

The parishioners murmuring words of blessings in chorus with most of their eyes closed. Asunder is flabbergasted. She picks up her bag and sneaks out from the crowd unseen.

PASTOR TYLER

Congratulations, Tchinda and Angel,
You have won this marriage battle,
Though the devil or his disciples rattle,
Like a rattlesnake, they're defeated.
Now you can be all seated.

PARISHIONERS

(In chorus)

Hallelujah!

Strings of music heard in the air, including the parishioners' yelling due to excitement. Then Pastor Tyler exits. On the other hand, Miss Asunder drives off from the church premises, parks in an isolated place not too far from her mansion and begins to weep.

MISS ASUNDER

Could James have betrayed me to Tyler?
His words were sharp, kind of an igniter,
Cutting through might heart with panic.
I hate him too; his words are volcanic
I will surely sink him too, like titanic.
I can't let Tchinda go; he's so romantic.
If he wants to obstruct my path so romantic
I don't think this game is already over,
I am not given up, too late to turn-over,
By hook or crook, I must take over.
Perhaps I should kill Angel if this works,
Now that I know she lives next blocks.

She lights treasurer luxury black cigarette and holds it between her lips, struggling to light.

MISS ASUNDER

(Continues)

Well—Angel, you're still a joker,
To think I will be here a lonely smoker.
You will end this game as a loser or loner.
Since you've made yourself an abuser,
Now people make me feel bad, the accuser.
I picked him at the airport, where were you?
Thief, a harlot, reaping where you did not sow.

There is an incoming call from Miss Beatrice.

MISS BEATRICE

Where are you? Where is your car?

We've been looking for you, girl!

MISS ASUNDER

I just drove off from the parking lot.
Trying to figure out hell for this harlot

MISS BEATRICE

Martin and I are here,
The D-day is fast running near,
We must do something to make it disappear.

MISS ASUNDER

Drive to my mansion; please come here,
Before heaven and hell, I swear,
That my wrath is kindle, Angel won't bear,
When I vomit on her since she adheres
To my husband as prey in a bear's,
Mouth struggling to survive in fears.

An hour later, Miss Beatrice, Miss Envy, and Mr. James enter Miss Asunder's mansion.

MISS BEATRICE

We are stepping up the game.
I care little now about my fame,
Yes, I care little; it's no longer a fair game.
This little brat has made me have all names,
But I want her to know that my last name,
Is unquenched fire.

MISS ASUNDER

We need a new phase,
So, we did bring a new face?
She's now in with James to erase,
Every bit of Angel, even ready to unlace
Her joy in church, or any other place.

MR. JAMES

A woman of her words, call her Envy,
She's my fiancé too, we all feel your pain,
We all feel how your heart is so heavy,
Your trust, money cannot be or go in vain.
Cheer up; she's omniscience, a member
Of the female planning committee, their leader,
Though young, she can influence an elder.

MISS ASUNDER

Does she know of the story's plot,
And what had at hand as a plot?

MISS ENVY

I am into it; I have been informed
Everything that now seems deformed,
Will soon get back its originality or form.
I can bring down fire and hailstorms,
That's how I can perform on any platform.

MISS BEATRICE

Goddess of destruction,
Rain on them, not only hailstorm,
Also rain, brim storm, thunderstorm,

Snowstorm, firestorm, ice storm, windstorm!

MISS ASUNDER

They have triggered my fire alarm,
They must pay for or be consumed.
This time around, I don't assume!

MISS BEATRICE

Any fixed date for the wedding?

MISS ENVY

Just in a month—

MISS ASUNDER

Let's have some Champaign,
Let's drink and sing a new song,
I can't wait to see them despair or rot
Rot under my fury, rot under my rod.

She turns on some classical music; they begin to celebrate.

MISS ASUNDER

Can a man take fire in his bosom,
And his clothes are not burnt?

MISS ASUNDER

Who dares!

MISS ASUNDER

Can one go upon hot coals,
And his feet are not burnt?

MISS ANVY

Who dares!

Mr. James and Miss Envy are to devise plans to confuse the wedding preparations. As members of the planning committee, they are closer to the target than Miss Asunder and Miss Beatrice.

ACT 6—SCENE 3

INT. CHURCH VICINITY - EVENING

After a church rehearsal session, James waits patiently for the performance to be over; then, he calls Mr. Tchinda aside. First tempter!

MR. JAMES

You're a gifted gift!

MR. TCHINDA

We're all part of the same body.

MR. JAMES

Do not forget;
Not all parts are the same!

MR. TCHINDA

That's true.
The less important shouldn't be less Important either.

MR. JAMES

Where is Miss Angel?
I did not see her for the rehearsals
This evening. Hope no recent reprisals?

There is an incoming text from Miss Angel to Tchinda.

MISS ANGEL

Honey,
I couldn't make it to the rehearsals.
I got stuck in traffic in Manhattan.
We meet at home, remain horny.
Love you!

MR. TCHINDA

She got stuck in traffic in Manhattan.

MR. JAMES

Have we got all the groomsmen for the wedding?

MR. TCHINDA

Yes, we, the men, are set.
Angel still needs one bridesmaid.
One just left, the who was her aids.

MR. JAMES

Hallelujah—brother!
That could be the devil one!

MR. TCHINDA

Who knows,
Now that the devil has crossed the line

MR. JAMES

They can cross,
But will never come across!

(Kissing a crucifix)

MR. TCHINDA

That's right, brother!
"*In hoc signo vinces*"

MR. JAMES

I can still remember,
Milvian Bridge battle

MR. TCHINDA

If a pagan like Flavius V. Constantine
Could wind with just a sign,
"In this sign conquer."
What more of we conquerors?

MR. JAMES

You're divinely right!
My fiancé can be a good bridesmaid's aid

MR. TCHINDA

Oh—really!

MR. JAMES

She's a good wedding planner!

MR. TCHINDA

We're blessed then!

MR. JAMES

Besides, elm—
I am somehow worried!

MR. TCHINDA

Worried!

MR. JAMES

I mean—disturbed!

MR. TCHINDA

Why?

MR. JAMES

The devil has crossed the battle line,
The Bible says he that finds a good Wife also obtains favor from God.

MR. TCHINDA

So—
Is Angel not favored to be my wife?

MR. JAMES

Not so—I didn't say that!

MR. TCHINDA

What then are you saying,
"What has Athens to do with Jerusalem"?

MR. JAMES

Please, don't misconstrue me.
It's just a concern, hoping you don't err!
You're a good soul, a perfect soul,
Good souls are not to be bruised by erred marriages.

MR. TCHINDA

Have I erred, or am I erring?

MR. TCHINDA

I'm persuaded—
Better a broken heart than marriage.

MR. TCHINDA

Now you speak like one of them,
Have you finally joined them?

MR. JAMES

Who are you referring to?

MR. TCHINDA

It is no longer a proverb—
The devils have crossed the battle line.

MR. JAMES

Are you now saying I am a devil?

MR. TCHINDA

The heart of man is desperately evil.
I didn't say you are. Are you?

MR. JAMES

Please make it not an offense.
I have cleared my mind from guilt,
I won't be part of this erring journey.

MR. TCHINDA

I am the traveler of this erring journey.

I have not retreated. Why would you surrender on my behalf? Shouldn't friends indeed be friends indeed?

MR. JAMES

We have been more than friends.

We're now brothers. How are we brothers When you see me as Esau after your life?

MR. TCHINDA

Did I say you're after my life?

MR. JAMES

Your wife, of course, is your life.

Hesitantly, he asks Mr. Tchinda for final prayers before they depart.

MR. JAMES

Well—If we aren't preyed,

Please pray for us to depart.

MR. TCHINDA

(now praying)

Father, I never knew hypocrisy—

Father, I never knew duplicity—

Until I became a Christian.

Deliver me, O Lord, that I be not like one of them. Amen!

MR. JAMES

Amen! Praying with cynicism?

MR. TCHINDA

Not sarcastic, was it?

You should not have said amen if it was. Everything is pure to them that are pure but defiled to them that are defiled.

Mr. James feels humiliated and disappointed. His plans have failed. He then exits. Mr. Tchinda is heard musing and mumbling Romans 7:14–25.

MR. TCHINDA

Help me, Lord,
If this be your will, as it is written,
"What you have put together,
Let no one put asunder."
Did I err? Isn't she the one?

EXIT

ACT 6—SCENE 4

INT. MISS ANGEL'S APARTMENT - EVENING

Miss Envy enters to help derail and cause doubts about Miss Angel's upcoming marriage. Mr. James has failed, and she is the only daring devil to cross the battle line.

MISS ENVY

Shalom!

MISS ANGEL

What a surprising visit?

MISS ENVY

I lost my phone and your contact,
I decided to stop by.

MISS ANGEL

I was about to call you.
Thanks for coming,
Thanks for being a divine aid

MISS ENVY

Iron sharpens iron.

MISS ANGEL

You're right!

MISS ENVY

You look so beautiful!
Where is your fiancé, Tchinda?
Is he at home at this moment?

MISS ANGEL

No!
He's still in church.

MISS ENVY

You're such a lucky angel.
How long have you known him?

MISS ANGEL

Years—let's say decades!
Though the path of love is rough!

MISS ENVY

Life is not a smooth journey.
If you are to make it honey,
You have to be ready with money.

MISS ANGEL

Money—
Its lust, the root to all evil.

MISS ENVY

Evil sometimes is indispensable.

Without evil, there is no righteousness. Without darkness, there is no light. Without disappointment, there's no appointment.

MISS ANGEL

Evil has crossed the battle line,

When they know they can't make it.

MISS ENVY

Life is a paradox.

Live it the way it comes.

The very angel you know can be an angel of darkness overnight. Be watchful, even for your upcoming wedding.

MISS ANGEL

You're rightly right.

Two days ago, I had a dream.

On our marital bed was a serpent forcing its way in between us.

MISS ENVY

Could that be a blunder to asunder?

MISS ANGEL

Well—

Whether a blunder to asunder

Or—asunder to blunder, I love him.

MISS ENVY

Love is blind, but don't be blind.
Love is patient, but not in asunder.
Why don't you look before leaping?

MISS ENVY

I have leaped already.
There's no time to look back.

MISS ENVY

Erring can be costly—
Costly means too expensive to repair.

MISS ANGEL

You're right, "If music be the food of love", we will play it on."
My lover will sing for me.
I will sing for him. Life rolls on.

MISS ENVY

Count me out!

MISS ANGEL

In or out does not change the battle line.

Miss Envy exits. Miss Angel is heard mumbling words of prayers. Mr. Tchinda then enters a few minutes after.

MISS ANGEL

Join me in prayers—
My soul is saddened.

MR. TCHINDA

Saddened is not hardened!

MISS ANGEL

The devils we knew have become demons.

MR. TCHINDA

Demons or devils, all are the same. If demons are everywhere, so are angels. You are one of these angels. In hell and in heaven, in fire or in water, we shall marry.

Miss Angel sobs and groans in Tchinda's arm. Night then falls.

Pleasing, seizing, freezing, and teasing;
Hissing, kissing, sneezing, wheezing
Intimacy, ultimacy, legitimacy, and intricacies
Complacency, vacancy, and intimacy;
Sweating, wetting, waiting, and petting
Thirty, thirsty, nasty, hasty, and tasty;
Rolling, blowing, groaning, and downing
Stroking, groping, chocking, and soaking.

NARRATOR

(Off Stage)

The rest is history.

EXIT

ACT 6—SCENE 5

INT. MISS ASUNDER'S MANSION - DAY

Miss Beatrice, Miss Envy, and Mr. James enter the apartment.

MISS ASUNDER

My heart within seems melting down.
My soul seems frozen and shutdown,
We can't fail; you can't let me down!

MR. JAMES

The wedding is in weeks downtown,
We can still try to turn it down.
Never too late for us to slow-down.

MISS BEATRICE

Impossible!
We will run them down,
We will crush them before sundown
Angel will not wear that bridal gown,
At all costs, she will be broken breakdown!

MISS ASUNDER

The clock is fast ticking,
I hear the sound of my rival groaning,
Whereas she's supposed to be mourning.

MR. JAMES

We sustain the air she breathes,
She can brag now but will soon be in grieves.

MISS ASUNDER

The battle might seem lost,
But not the war ahead is a win-win!
We'll win at all costs, despite any cost!
She'll see another side to the holocaust.

MISS BEATRICE

We'll fight this war altogether,
Altogether we'll stand—no retreat ever,
Till the war is fought and victory forever!

MR. JAMES

I know retreat, no surrender!

MISS BEATRICE

He's a man of soft heart—tenderness.
That's his only flaw, too compassionate,
We'll frame him up, get him to the wilderness,
Then he will give up hope once helpless.

MISS ASUNDER

How?

MISS BEATRICE

Call and stage a phone drama,
Tell him I am in a coma,
Then drop—

MISS ENVY

I am not sure he'll be nudged,
He might know the story is forged.

MISS BEATRICE

Worry not, I know him so well
He won't only be nudged but touched.
Every tragic hero has a weakness or spell,
That will lead to his downfall or hell.
Once down, we can have him squashed or crushed.

MISS ASUNDER

What are we supposed to do once here,
It's a good plan, but I am still unclear.

MISS BEATRICE

Satan offered Jesus worldly pleasure,
When he comes, offer him your treasure,
Propose him sex—

MISS ASUNDER

This has never worked in the past,
Neither is he going to fall any fast.

MISS BEATRICE

The past is past!
This time is by hook or crook,
He will be at all cost hooked.
If he denies or tries to overlook,
Then we take the devil alternative.

MISS ASUNDER

It sounds like a plan!

MISS BEATRICE

Sex and blackmail are what we need,
To force him to comply or his misdeed,
Will be used against him as a stampede.

Mr. James and Miss Envy are nodding in approval.

MISS BEATRICE

We shall take a retreat in the guest room.
If he falls prey, then he is preyed on forever.
This will mar him from being Angel's groom.
He will be yours for live and whenever.

MISS ASUNDER

What if he doesn't fall prey?

MISS BEATRICE

Well—strip yourself naked
If he denies or is not still persuaded,
Then scream for rape, roll on the ground,
Then we'll come out and take pictures,
That will be used in the court of law…

MISS ASUNDER

Who takes the pictures?

MR. JAMES

I will!

MISS ENVY

Not you!
What do you want to see?

MISS ASUNDER

I am desperate! I don't mind to sacrifice Jerusalem's sight for the salvation of Tchinda. Of what importance has it been all this while?

MISS ENVY

I will do it.
There is nothing new under the sun!

Miss Asunder is dialing Tchinda's number. There's silence in every corner of her mansion. After the second and third attempts, he still does not pick up. Miss Asunder gets frustrated with cracks on her face.

MR. JAMES

Why don't you send him a text?
He might be in church?

MISS ASUNDER

(texting with trembling hands)

Hoping he sees the text and calls me back.
Tchinda calls back while she is still texting.

MR. TCHINDA

Hello!

Miss Asunder is yelling on the other end of the phone as a professional mourner, not giving any chance for Tchinda to ask questions. He forcefully and cunningly drops the call after jostling some words.

MR. TCHINDA

Talk to me. What's going on?

MISS ASUNDER

Miss Beatrice is unconscious.

Please haste over!

Miss Asunder hangs up the phone. Miss Envy, Miss Beatrice, and Mr. James enter the guest room.

ACT 7—SCENE 1

INT. MISS ASUNDER'S MANSION - DAY

Mr. Tchinda enters fifteen minutes later.

MR. TCHINDA

What calls an emergency
That requires me with immediacy,
When I do see nothing worth urgency,
Hope there's no insurgency?

MISS ASUNDER

Brave coward, do you see insurgency?
I am giving you my last courtesy,
For us to sort out our final divergency,
We've long been in this idiosyncrazy,
Which is now driving me so crazy.

MR. TCHINDA

An angel of light, a well-known daisy,
Why is your evil heart so racy?
Why have you sold your heart without mercy?
Your heart is now the devil's triangle,
Your heart is now the limbo of the death,
Your heart is now the twilight zone,
Your heart is now a hoodoo sea

Your heart is now a Bermuda Triangle
Why such evil, would you harbor in vain?

MISS ASUNDER

I am glad you know my other names,
I am glad you know I fit in all frames,
You've called me the Bermuda Triangle,
But you've dared my enchanted island,
You've proven braved to the cahow's call
To venture where others did try and fall.
We're in a sinking ship, with the same storm
Where we must survive at all cost—best
Known to none only to us, no-one else!
We've long acted our drama on stage,
Now, we have to act drama off stage

Asunder strips herself naked. Her dress and bra torn in tags.

Come on in and eat!
Eat of wild fruits of the fairest jungle,
I am still very much patient and humble,
To invite you, to my enchanted island,
Be bold, do not dread, do not grumble,
Some chances are rare to see or stumble
Upon. Would you again deny it?

MR. TCHINDA

Lucifer! Satan! Get behind me!

MISS ASUNDER

Please, keep religion aside or outside,
We know it's meant for cowards, besides,

I know you aren't one of them- so to speak,
Sweat poet, I am getting horny to its peak.
Give it to me once, and your angel twice!
Let me have it just once, then your angel twice.

MR. TCHINDA

Neither an iota nor ounce!

MISS ASUNDER

(attempting to seduce Tchinda)

I have the keys to both hell and heaven,
Nobody resists and survives in my Bermuda,
To give some insight, poet from Bamenda,
In a post-feminist sue-happy society,
I have the law in between my legs, "pica."
I can promote and demote anyone with no grunt.
Be wise; take advantage of this piety.

MR. TCHINDA.

Villainous villain!
You so belittle the US Congress,
Its laws to your "coochie," for evil's progress?

MISS ASUNDER

Mr. Poet, you're not a lawyer.
Besides, there is evil behind every law.
That's why we are here; I am the law.
What my coochie can't do, the law will do.
What the law can't do, my coochie will do.

MR. TCHINDA

You can make the law look so corrupt,
You can seek to have the law disrupt,
Other's peace and happiness, or interrupt,
Their freedom to equality and liberty,
You might even use the law trying to irrupt,
My love for Angel, as you plan to obstruct.
The law and the congress can only imprison
My body, but they can't imprison my love,
They can't imprison my heart to Angel.
Note that, to every treason without reason,
Theirs is punishment or chastisement.
You might pride in its beginning merriment,
The end shall speak for itself with no sentiment.

MISS ASUNDER

Well said;
I know you're a drammarian,
I am neither one nor grammarian!
All I need is you and you alone!
Give to Caesar what belongs to him.

MR. TCHINDA

Well said Angel is my Caesar!
Or are you also a Caesarian,
To know who's Caesar, and who isn't!

MISS ASUNDER

I am more than a Caesarian,
I am a vulgarian cesarian!

MR. TCHINDA

Cesarians are humanitarians,
Not dehumanitarians!

MISS ASUNDER

Have you forgotten parliamentarian?
I have changed seasons and times,
Since the 1950s, I am a new law,
The new law, I am the new Jim Crow
A Jim Crow post-feminist who can crow
At all times and not sometimes.
We are a sue-happy society, with no piety,
We can play it in cash, in-kind, or by law!

MR. TCHINDA

Can I restroom your restroom?

MISS ASUNDER

Of course,
You're free to restroom the restroom!
I will also presume or do assume,
Your epididymis is now ready to comply.
Let me offer my generosity to your peristalsis,
To dissolve the fire within or crises,
I am ready to gargle your payload, spooge,
Candy cream, meat milk, willy tease.
Till you circumjaculate or circumambulate.
Just know I love eating carrots,
Just know I love smoking the pole,
Just know I love complimenting the chief.
Just know I love knights of the round table.

MR. TCHINDA

Jezebel!

Tchinda goes to the bathroom to turn on his recorder. Beatrice then enters the living room, unknown to Tchinda. While inside the restroom, he talks to himself in front of the bathroom mirror.

MR. TCHINDA

(soliloquy)

"To be or not to be."
To do or not to do?
Here's my dilemma!

Tchinda re-enters into the living room.

MR. TCHINDA

Now I see the gang,
Brood of vampires!

MISS BEATRICE

I proposed to you all the empires,
I forewarned of this Armageddon.
Didn't I?

MR. TCHINDA

You villain, your villainy is vain.

MISS ASUNDER

Now I have a witness to my case.
Let's play it low once and for all.
Threesome? We're ready for you; any pace,

If you cannot love me for my skin color, At least across colors, sex tastes the same,
In Europe, America, or any other place.

TCHINDA

Rust and rest in hell!

MISS ASUNDER

We're already in hell,
Can hell be hotter than a broken heart?

MR. TCHINDA

You've slain many by the law,
You've made evil reside behind the law. The law has authority over my flesh.
It can slay my flesh to rest and rust,
It can't muzzle the conscience of justice in me.

Miss Asunder slaps Tchinda, took her phone, and dials 911.

MISS ASUNDER

Son of a bitch, S.O.B!
I hate you—a rapist. Help me!

Miss Asunder and Miss Beatrice struggling to wrestle Tchinda to the floor. Then four policemen enter. Tchinda is now on the floor restrained. He is apprehended.

POLICE

Is he the rapist?

MISS ASUNDER

He is!

Tchinda is arrested and is escorted to the police station.

ACT 7—SCENE 2

NARRATOR
(Off Stage)

I'm in doubts in our systems called justice and laws
I support fair systems called justice and laws.
What manmade is fallible and full of flaws,
Some laws, are more deadly than a chainsaw,
The innocents are convicted and detained raw,
Let me tell a story, as once invited to witness a trial,
The accuser was a cat, the chief judge a big cat,
The accused was colored, innocent, and was a rat.
In such a case, we know the answer, what's next?
Evil resides behind the law, used by some as a pretext
To elude justice, don't be perplexed
The world in which we are, lawlessness favoritism,
A form of democracy or congressional solecism.

There is too much injustice; barbarism called racism.
Let's be steadfast, hold our breath, and braced,
Let's watch the ordeal of these lovers as they face
A crime not committed, a society of justice misplaced.
We're to the mercy of the law, as we run this race,
When lawmakers are big cats, when judges are big cats,
What becomes of colored rats, who face their lambaste
With no parole, no voice to look into their disgraced?

Let' have our fingers crossed for Tchinda and Angel,
Hope the judge be a good big cat with discretion,
To see evil behind the law or bring peace and recreation.

We need to rethink, slow down, and not in haste,
The law has done us harm; lives are a waste,
I might not believe in our justice, nor have a lawless nation,
But we must together stand for the law in a system
To decry vice in truth, not applaud evil in judicial ovation.
Every life matters, black lives like other lives,
We're all pilgrims and must have a heart that forgives,
A heart to build one dream and one nation with caution.
Let's, not our ego—selfish desires become laws of negation
To think for others and have others think of themselves less
In our so-called litigation, racial justice of condemnation,
Let's not conclude the end; let's keep steadfast admiration
For our hero who strives to survive in social ruination
For the sake of a woman he loves in truth, not segregation
I have much in mind, both in acclamation and summation,
I am like a woman in gestation with much anticipation.

INT. COURT HOUSE, NEW YORK - ANGEL'S WEDDING DAY - EVENING

Pastor Tyler is seated in front of the court, closer to the judgment box. Miss Angel is leaning on his shoulder, weeping for consolation. Parishioners and the choir are all well dressed, seated behind pastor Tyler. Mr. James and Miss Envy are standing outside the courtroom, spying from the window. Then Miss Asunder, Miss Beatrice, Asunder's lawyer, Mr. Tchinda in handcuffs, and law enforcement officers enter.

POLICE

Court, rise!

Judge Justice enters the court.

JUDGE JUSTICE

Swear by this Holy Bible to say the truth
And only truth in this court!

TCHINDA

I promise to tell the truth,
All the truth for the truth,
And by the truth, I stand truthful.

MISS ASUNDER

I pledge to the truth!

JUDGE JUSTICE

If found guilty for either;

First, second, third- or fourth-degree rape, Under the New York Penal Code, Section 130.05—130.96; You will be imprisoned,

Or sentenced from five years minimum up to twenty-five years maximum.

Now looking at the accuser, Judge Justice orders Miss Asunder to present her case.

MISS ASUNDER

After work, so unfateful that evening,
He came to my mansion so overweening.
I had just taken a shower, dressed in nighty

Ready to go to bed, came a knock so mighty,
On my door, echoing and yelling my name.
I recognized his voice, though not his aim,
For such a nocturnal visit, so unexpected.
I gave him food to eat, wine to drink,
After eating and drinking, I noticed him erect,
I remained calm, sober with all respect.
He called me honey, said he was horny,
I gave him deaf ears; he did smile and blink,
Then he said to me; he wanted us to have sex.

(Begins crying pretentiously, courthouse murmuring)

I refused; my religion does not allow sex,
Before marriage, but he tried another pretext,
Said, "it's freezing outside," but good inside,
How's it, if we slept side by side, or beside?
One another, hugging, kissing, teasing
Blissing, blessing, cissing, missing, wissing,
Stripping, tripping, spitting, sleeping, sipping,
Impress, caress, redress, undress, process
Progress, transgress, suppress, repress,

To all this, I said, he forcedly began groping

JUDGE JUSTICE

Have you been dating or in a relationship?

MISS ASUNDER

Never! Not my type,
He's not worth my hype!

JUDGE JUSTICE

According to your report or file,
Beatrice came in so abruptly on time?
She refrained him for a while.
You called 911. Is this true?

MISS ASUNDER

Yes, very true!
(courthouse murmuring)

JUDGE JUSTICE

Quiet!
Where is Beatrice?

Miss Beatrice raises her hand, and the judge calls her forward to testify.

JUDGE JUSTICE

Can you attest to this?

MISS BEATRICE

I happened to have stopped at her house,
From outside, was a noise like a clubhouse,
She helpless, pleading and begging,
I heard his voice, heartless and bragging,
While she wailed or wept not to be raped.
The door was opened, I then intruded
She was entirely naked, extruded, stranded.

Miss Beatrice opens her handbag and Asunder's nude picture which she has printed from her phone. A female court attendant takes them to one of the female judges for review. Turning to Tchinda, Judge Justice asks reluctantly, with a voice of conviction from Miss Beatrice and Miss Asunder's testimony.

JUDGE JUSTICE

Two voices have spoken,
What else, can you be outspoken?

MR. TCHINDA

False and fake!

JUDGE JUSTICE

At least you went to her residence.
Any counterevidence!

Mr. Tchinda puts his hand in his jacket pocket and brings out his phone. The court is quiet. All eyes are watching, and ears are eager to hear. Looking up to the judge, he pauses, clears his throat, then begins to play the entire story on a loudspeaker. The court attendance, yelling, and Miss Angel is soaked with tears.

MR. TCHINDA

If the only crime in this crime is this,
I fell in love with the woman I love
And will marry and merry,
And if loving her is a crime,
Then let me be a criminal for her Love.
I have only one life to live on earth.
I have only one person to love on earth.
And I have only one heart to love on earth.

And only one person can enter,
This one heart here on earth—Miss Angel.
How can a man with only one heart
In the same heart, love two women?

AUDIENCE

Unfair fairness!

MR. TCHINDA

Are of such things, black codes laws,
Now in our nation, by Congress,
To convict two lovers for loving each other?

The audience are now murmuring.

MR. TCHINDA

Are of such things, black codes laws,
Now in our nation, by Congress
Stating that a man must pay a fine for loving and not being loved?

The audience are again murmuring.

MR. TCHINDA

Have I sinned in this scene?
The only sin I have seen is the sin of love. Let Miss Angel and myself be confined in a holy matrimony, as the fine for a sin is neither sinned nor defined.

JUDGE JUSTICE

(furiously staring at the accusers)

The accuser, any objection?

Miss Beatrice and Miss Asunder are all silent, feeling guilty.

JUDGE JUSTICE

Where is Miss Angel?
Is she in this courtroom?
Let her stand up and come in front.

Pastor Tyler helps gather her wedding or long bridal gown from the ground. He supports Miss Angel as they both walk in front.

JUDGE JUSTICE

(continues)

Miss Angel, please take heart!
The allegation against your fiancé is false! He's not guilty!

Hugging Tchinda in the judgement box, she looks into his eyes, blushing, as tears crawl on her cheek. Then she begins to speak.

MISS ANGEL
The Law and the Conscience

In every nation,
There is a constitution.
In this constitution,
There is a book.
In this book,
There is the law.
In these laws,
There is a law—
The supreme law.
Over these supreme laws,
There are judges.

Amongst these judges,
There is a judge—
The supreme, my Lord
To him belongs the last verdict.

Every man is a whole nation.
In every man,
There is a constitution.
In this constitution,
There is a holy book.
In this holy book,
There are laws.
In these laws,
There is a supreme law—
The law of the conscience.
Over these laws,
We all are judges.
Among us, the judges,
There is a supreme judge—
The judge of the conscience.
To him belongs the last verdict.

Every judge has a supreme judge.
Every unjust judge who judges
Shall also be judged unjustly by a judge
In the supreme and incorruptible court—
That of the conscience.

JUDGE JUSTICE

Do you wish to press any charges against Miss Asunder and Miss Beatrice for the damages they caused you on your wedding day?

MR. TCHINDA
A New City Upon the Hill, America

God, in the beginning, was America.
America was with God,
And God was America.

God never created America,
He will never ask of America
Of Americans,
But He will ask of Americans of America.
You and I, both president and citizen,
The change we brought to Washington
And not the change Washington brought to us.

Are you American?
Because you were born in America,
Or because America is born in you,
You are American?

God will never look for Americans
In America, but He will look for America
In every American.

To be born in America
Or to have given birth to America
Does not make you either American.

Every American
Is any man, black or white,
Who knows what to say,
What to do to defend its colors.

The American Head of State is no American,
But every American is the head of states.
If all our hope is looking up
To the head of state for change,
And all Americans are the state,
Then we are the source of our hope and change.

Stop asking what Washington will bring to you,
And start asking what you can bring to Washington.
No American was ever born in Washington,
But Washington was born in every American:
You and I, president or citizen.

Lord, restore this city upon the hill.
Lord, restore the city upon the hill.
Lord, restore America.
God bless—America.
Long live—America.

JUDGE JUSTICE

I hereby declare Miss Asunder guilty
Of and for being the evil behind the law,
Tarnishing the image of our nation
That was built on the blood of martyrs.
The Bill of Rights, or defense of women's rights
Was never passed to promote evil,
But for justice to prevail against evil.

Women and men, blacks and whites,
Have equal rights before the law,
To love and to inter-marry.
Against which miscegenation laws are

Outlawed in our nation, Loving v. Virginia,
And shall not be judged by the color of their skins,
But by the content of their character and hearts.
The feminist law was not meant to be a threat to us,
But we are threats to these laws and society,
No evil behind the law will go unpunished.

Pastors Tyler, the church attendants, and other court attendants are rejoicing.

JUDGE JUSTICE

(Continues)

We shall all stand before this court and witness the wedding of Miss Angel and Mr. Tchinda unfold as a reality.

Miss Angel's bridesmaids, the girl of honor, enter the court from behind. The groomsmen are all dressed so colorfully. They march into the court in a linear motion. Pastor Tyler then gets his Bible for the benediction.

PASTOR TYLER

(Continues)

Is there anybody here who has any reason Why these two lovers should not mingle?

The court is in a clamor.

PASTOR TYLER

Miss Angel,
Do you accept him as your wedded husband?

MISS ANGEL

For eternity, prosperity, and posterity.

PASTOR TYLER

Mr. Tchinda,
Do you accept Angel as your wedded wife?

MR. TCHINDA

If love is a sacrilege,
Let me consume hers as a privilege.

PASTOR TYLER

You can now kiss your bride.

MR. TCHINDA

(whispering in Miss Angel's ear)

Some kisses are for the public.
Others are reserved for private use only.

COURT AUDIENCE

(yelling)

Romeo and Juliet! Tchinda and Angel!

PASTOR TYLER

Peter Abelard and Héloïse!

While hugging both lovers, Judge Justice officially declares them as husband and wife.

JUDGE JUSTICE

Miss Beatrice and Miss Asunder will have to face criminal charges.

Four policemen enter. They handcuff Miss Beatrice and Miss Asunder and take them out of the courtroom.

ACT 7—SCENE 3

NARRATOR

(Off Stage)

Let it be so; if love is a crime, let him be a criminal,
Let it be so; if love is a crime, let her be a criminal.
When a man's heart is certainly curtained and love arrest,
What else is left than to consume it for pleasure and rest?
Love begins as a feeling; we live to fight for and profess,
It goes beyond just words; there is more to see in a love nest,
Of course, some know what I mean, or I have to say so pressed,
The final stage of love, you moan and groan, not in distress
Does better to the soul and to the mind, for it's the ultimate rest,
For which Miss Asunder had long desired, till she got vexed,
I wish this couple the best, as I know they are blessed.
They have gone through the test of time, I must confess,
I watched them in sorrow; I watched them in tears contest,
To preserve that which they cherished most in social unrest,
Of human cruelty and the law, the evil we all sometimes ingest
In our desperate attempts to make our needs or desperate quest
To use our race power, to conquer the weak in greed or prowess.
Now that I know there are godly cats and ungodly rats,
We all have a task at hand to look out for evil brats
Whose skin color takes pride in the law to suppress or behest
The poor in spirit. I now am glad, no more pain unexpressed.

EXT. OUTSIDE THE COURT - NEW YORK CITY – EVENING

MR. TCHINDA

Where would you want us to spend our honeymoon?

MRS. ANGEL

Somewhere in the moon, I guess,
Where we will have no guest,
Where there is time to jest or rest.
No invite, except the stars our nest
As we jest and rest in our love nest.

MR. TCHINDA

Oh yes!
What I waited for years.
Venus as bright as your vena amoris.

MRS. ANGEL

Has love made you a Latin poet?
We've eaten enough poetry and drama in Courtship. Let amoris wait aside or outside.
I am famished for the love—
The one I have stood for,
The one I have worked for,
The one merit.

INT. HONEYMOON NIGHT – LATE EVENING

MRS. ANGEL

(Continues)

Why are you gazing at my fingers?
Aren't you the one who bought the ring?

MR. TCHINDA

Vena Amoris connects your finger,
Directly to your heart.

MRS. ANGEL

Okay.
I have heard you.
What else do you want to tell me?

MR. TCHINDA

Of course, you are so pretty.

MRS. ANGEL

Is that why we are married, pretty?

MR. TCHINDA

You're pretty, and I'm not guilty.

MRS. ANGEL

Stop flatteries!

MR. TCHINDA

(in poesy oration)

Beauty and Love

Women's love and beauty
Are in a pot of flowers kept.
When they fall in love
And when they truly fall to love,
They make a choice of a flower
And colors.

You who say you truly love me,
With which flower and color
Do you love me?

You who say you truly love me,
With the best of your flowers
And colors,
Why and for whom
Do you still keep the other flowers
And colors?

You who say you truly love me,
With all the best of your flowers,
With all the best of your colors,
Why and for whom
Do you still keep your garden?

You who promised me your love,
Will you give me
Your best flower and color?
Or will you give me
All your best flowers and colors?
Or will you give me your entire
Garden of flowers and colors?

MRS. ANGEL

I have given you the entire garden.
I have given you the flowerpot.
I have given you the flower.
I have given you the best color.
What else do you want?

MR. TCHINDA

I am in love.

MRS. ANGEL

Now that you're in love, if you ever cheat on me—I will call 911!

Now that you're in love, if you ever dream of any woman in your dream—I will call 911!

Now that you're in love, if you ever talk when I am talking—I will call 911!

Now that you're in love, if you ever sneeze without permission—I will call 911!

Now that you're in love, if I need marital cake and you are not in the mood—I will call 911.

Now that you're in love, the day I prepare food without salt, and you complain— I will call 911!

Now that you're in love, when you work, I will be the one to cash your salary.

If you complain—I will call 911!

MR. TCHINDA

(Aside)

From one prison to the other!

LIGHTS OFF

Pause—Wait!

Lights, alight, faintly, fading,
Undress, access, assess,
Press, unstressed, caress,
Yes, impress, unrest,
Finest, nobles, excess.

Breast, bleat, bleed,
Bare, bear, blare,
Blessed night!
Blessed knight!

Grinning, grunting, groaning,
Meeting, making, mating,
Dreaming, drowning, droning,
Moaning, owning, rolling,
Shocking, sobbing, socking,
Singing, hissing, kissing,
Kidding, dancing, teasing,
Seizing, easing, wheezing.

Pennies, promise, premise,
Home rest, honest, love nest
Caress, obsess, profess.

Years, yes, yours,
Forever, never, over,
Best, bet, better.

EPILOGUE

Love Is Nothing but Poetry, Prose, and Drama

Sweet and fair lady,
Come forth, being ready
In this lonesome garden,
With all the glory of Eden
And let's disco to this melody.
Love is drama; some act it as comedy,
While others believe it is a tragedy or parody.

Sweet and fair lady,
Come forth, being ready
That we disco to this melody
A drama of tragicomedy.
Bewitch me not in that attire
Whose beneath beauty is a rhetoric
Lest I am confused and tell you in my poetic
I love you, whereas I meant to say a satire.

Your face is prettier when you smile;
Perhaps a metaphor or simply a simile.
Love is the only confused confusion
Whose dramatic name can be called allusion.
Of great heroes who fell in love but in illusion
Like King Solomon, who, in his point of view,
Lamented a thousand women he knew

And wrote good alliteration in repetition.

Sweet and fair lady,
Come forth, being ready,
Let's turn this garden into a metaphor.
Let's dance until dawn, and live by this irony
Love is blind, let's call the night a personification.
Let's personify the irony and call it agony.

O sweet lady, what then is love?
A fool once fell in love
And said, "All fools are wise."
A wise man once fell in love
And said, "All wise men are fools."
A poet once fell in love
And said, "Love is the beauty
Of art, and the art of beauty."
That is seen in scenes and acts
As a melody, comedy, parody,
Tragicomedy, satire, rhetoric,
Simile, metaphor, allusion, repetition,
Irony and personification.

LIGHTS OFF - END

NARRATOR'S FINAL REMARKS - EULOGY

Let the palm wine flow and kola nut speak.
Our ancestors are gone; others are sick.
Our mother, at her old age, still has virgin breasts.
The breasts that fed you all till you went to rest.

We're all product of colonial rape.
She's raped at gunpoint and fed with wild grapes.
Bleeding and pleading for her children's sake.
Year after, like a goat, she has been bleating.

It wasn't a fault of hers that the Versailles Treaty
Forced upon her two suitors, Britain and France.
She was betrothed without libation.
Bole Butake, one of her children, saw this struggle.

They'd freely enjoyed our mother's virginity,
Found pleasure in her groans and saw no cruelty.
Bate Bisong, may your soul rest in peace.
Her offspring have been treated with unfairness penalty,
Like a *Beasts of No Nation*, seeking for a new nation.
Mongo Beiti, Eza Boto, or Alexandre Biyidi Awala,
We, your children, need a new *Mission to Kala*.
The "Jean-Marie Medza" is waiting for your blessing.

We are *No Longer at Ease* at home.
Please, Chinua Achebe, let our ancestors know.

My younger sister is jobless after college.
Corruption has become our national language.
Ngugi wa Thiong'o and Ngugi wa Mirii
Have been soothing her with her best comrade, Gathoni,
"I Will Marry When I Want" because she feels at ease
Since "The Beautiful Ones Are Not Yet Born."
Thanks to Ayi Kwei Armah for his comforting words also.

Bernard Fonlon, we'd taught the national anthem,
Peace-Work-Fatherland, in both English and French.
Today, your children are tired.
They all fear for their lives if they sing in the "Amba land."
Saint Exupery called it "Terre Des Hommes."

If you sing, you'll be *Murder in the Cathedral*
Like Archbishop Thomas Becket, Thomas T. Eliot.
What a pity for our world! Christ, save us!
My elder brother has become the *Mayor of Casterbridge*.
Thomas Hardy, also knows him very well.
He now also behaves like same colonial rapist
And does not care about *Black Boy* anymore,
Even if he hears the voice of Richard Wright calling.

We still have few brave orators like
Kashim Tala Ibrahim, *Orature in Africa*,
Who still speaks with integrity to his sons,
Enongene Sone, in proverbs, riddles, or call it palm oil
With which words are eaten.

Another baobab tree three had recently fallen,
Prutus Tawang Tah, The Immortal Seed,
Single tree in the forest, that could be a forest by himself.
He's now with Linus T. Asong,

Who finished his martyred race with a "crown of thorns."
Shadrach Ambanasom, a true *Son of the Native Soil*,
Safe journey.

Pray for your sons who are now leaving their native home To find comfort in the hands of strange mother.

Ferdinand Oyono warned them not to be a *Houseboy*,
But they kept dreaming like *The Old Man and the Medal.*
Some have lost hope and fallen in love, like Miss Asunder.
In Tchinda F. Mbuna's *The Evil Behind the Law*,
Ngũgĩ a Thiong'o' said it right, *Weep Not, Child.*

Only children dream to be like *Romeo and Juliet.*
They follow William Shakespeare and pretend to be
Sons and Lovers as D. H. Lawrence, but they forget that
There is a price to pay, or their lives become
Robert Sheridan's *School for Scandal.*

Sons of the Native Soil have suffered Christ-like.
Other's gone through *The Trials of Brother Jero*, but
Wole Soyinka did not relent.

Now I cry from a foreign land with Miss Angel.
There is *Evil Behind the Law.*
Everyone now sings, Black Lives Matter,

Like Barack Obama's tale, *A Story of Race and Inheritance*, deeply rooted in *Dreams from My Father.*

Some have forsaken their dreams,
"A Midsummer Night's Dream."
Some dream because others dream,
Behold the Dreamers, Imbolo Mbue,
True daughter of Zion, had seen it too.
How Beautiful We Were is now rhetoric to others.

"I can't Breathe," we can't wait no more.
"The Negro Is Your Brother" Martin Luther,
Prophet of American Civil Right Movements,
Predicted, but was called unwise and untimely.
Today, we still sing the same song,
"I can't breathe," Black Lives Matter.

Is time we dare to rise with *The Audacity of Hope*,
Yes, "We Can;" "A Promised Land" promise,
"Of thee I Sing" a new patriotic song.
"A Letter to my Daughters," "The Negro Is Your Brother,"
"Letter from Birmingham Jail, Letter from Birmingham City Jail," "Injustice anywhere, a threat to justice everywhere."

Where Do We Go from Here: Chaos or Community?
"We Need Strength to Love" and to be born again.
There's evil behind the law that's *Why We Can't Wait*.
We need to *Stride for Freedom: Montgomery Story.*
There's a divine "Call to Conscience" and justice for
Christopher Lowe, Javier Ambler II, Derrick Scott,
Byron Williams, John Elliott Neville, Manuel Ellis,
George Floyd, inter alia.

It's time for *The Trumpet of Conscience.*
It's time we all say, "I Have a Dream."
It's time we know righteousness or *All Labor Has Dignity*.
It's time we know "We Are Tied to a Single Garment of Destiny."
The Measure of a Man is not in supremacist ideology,
But the "content of their character."

I need to breathe; I need to breathe freely.
I need love; I need to be loved freely.
I need freedom; I need freedom freely.

GLOSSARY

Achu: A West African dish, mostly known in Cameroon

Ange: French word for Angel

Bamenda: A town in the northern region of Cameroon

Bermuda Triangle: Known to be a mysterious place in the western part of the North Atlantic Ocean

Cahow: A bird often associated with the myth of the Bermuda Triangle

In hoc signo vinces*: In this sign, conquer*

Jollof: A West African dish

Quenceess: Compound word for queen and princess

Soya/Suya. This is a form of grilled meat (Soya in Cameroon and Suya in Nigerian English).

Water Fufu or Eru: A West African dish, mostly known in Cameroon

Confuzzle: Compound words from confused and puzzle

REFERENCES

1. Smith, P. G. et al, *The Sheldon Book of Verse,* Oxford University Press: London, 1988, P. 132.

2. Sampson, Nkwetatang, *Discourses,* Magnolian Publishers : Bamenda, 2013, P. 49.

3. Hughes, Langston, *An African Treasury*, Pyramid Publishers: USA, 1970, P. 74.

4. Blunden, Edmund, *Selected Poems of Tennyson*, Heinemann Educational Books Ltd: London, P. 36.

5. Shakespeare, W, *The Tragedy of Romeo and Juliet,* CreateSpace Independent Publishing Platform, February 22, 2013.

6. Sone, E. M. (n.d.), *Globalization And Cameroon Oral Literature: Calamity Or Cure?*

7. Thiong'o, N. W., *The River Between (African Writers Series) 1st Edition,* Heinemann, August 11, 2008.

EXAMINATION QUESTIONS

1. In your opinion, would you classify this play as a fictional or true-life story? Why?
2. Why is the author of this play a poet, but he has written a play rather than a poetry book?
3. Is it righteous for Mr. Tchinda and Miss Angel to live together in the same house before ever getting married?
4. Is Miss Asunder truly in love with Mr. Tchinda?
5. Does true love without material interest still exist in present-day society?
6. What part does Mr. James play in this play, and how does it contribute to the plot's development?
7. Is Pastor Tyler a genuine man of God? Why?
8. Why is the author of this play one of the actors in the play?
9. What makes us believe that the author of this play is a Cameroonian?
10. Is this play a comedy, or is it a tragedy?
11. What do you think happened to Miss Asunder and Mr. James?
12. Do you think or accept there injustice or evil lurking behind our law system?

WATCH OUT FOR VOLUME 2 AND 3…